Introduction to
Reference and Information Services
in Today's School Library

Introduction to Reference and Information Services in Today's School Library

Lesley S. J. Farmer

ROWMAN & LITTLEFIELD
Lanham • Boulder • New York • Toronto • Plymouth, UK

Published by Rowman & Littlefield
4501 Forbes Boulevard, Suite 200, Lanham, Maryland 20706
www.rowman.com

10 Thornbury Road, Plymouth PL6 7PP, United Kingdom

British Library Cataloguing in Publication Information Available

Library of Congress Cataloging-in-Publication Data

Farmer, Lesley S. J.
Introduction to reference and information services in today's school library / Lesley S.J. Farmer.
pages cm
Includes bibliographical references and index.
ISBN 978-0-8108-9309-2 (cloth : alk. paper) — ISBN 978-0-8108-8718-3 (pbk.) — ISBN 978-0-
8108-8719-0 (ebook)
1. School libraries—Reference services. I. Title.
Z675.S3F2366 2014
025.5'2778—dc23
2013040895

Printed in the United States of America

To my professors at UNC Chapel Hill and my colleagues at Baltimore County Public Library, who started me on my reference career.

Contents

Preface

Do school libraries need to provide reference and information services in this digital age? Isn't everything already available for anyone to find and use? Aren't today's students tech-savvy enough to navigate this cyber world? The answers are "Yes," "No," and "No."

In most cases, the big issue isn't find a piece of information; it's finding the right information—and knowing what to do with it. Students have difficulty evaluating and valuing information. Today's students may use lots of social media for personal needs, but those skills are not transferring well to academic arenas. Students have little idea about the information universe and how to match their information needs with different knowledge representations.

School library programs provide rich cross-curricular information experiences, guided by tech-savvy school librarians. School librarians provide organized collections of professionally selected refererence resources, and they offer access to a world of digital references as well. They know how to locate and use reference sources to meet the information needs of the school community, and they teach the school community those skills.

Introduction to Reference and Information Services in Today's School Library reconceptualizes references and information services (RIS) in light of today's information universe, emerging technologies, informational needs, and students. Each chapter focuses on one aspect of RIS, and the book weaves in assessment and strategies throughout.

WHAT'S IN STORE

The first chapter defines information and its world, information seekers, and the role of school librarians in that world to provide reference and information services.

The second chapter points out the need to start assessing the school community and determining what services can be provided with existing resources. The assessment can also determine what RIS services might be marketed, and what resources or services could be added or redirected.

The third chapter discusses different information behaviors, drawing upon current theories. It then provides techniques for effectively researching and retrieving information from different types of print, nonprint, and digital resources.

Chapter 4 focuses on reference sources that meet school community needs. Specific criteria, for different formats and populations, are noted. The chapter lists core reference resources at different school levels.

The fifth chapter deals with physical access to reference and other information resources. It discusses issues of arrangement, cataloging, virtual access, and disability requirements.

Chapter 6 conceptualizes reference interviews as information conversation and interaction in order to emphasize the process as a negotiated and partnership model. The chapter notes standards and strategies for reference interactions, in both face-to-face and virtual settings. Consortia and outsourced digital reference services are also examined.

The seventh chapter addresses the core function of instruction. The chapter begins by listing information literacy standards, then details instructional design, which offers a systematic way to approach information instruction. It gives ideas for different modes of instruction and ways to embed instruction into the curriculum.

Curation, the selection and organization of information, has become a popular value-added information function. The eighth chapter discusses the process of curating and designing information packages, addressing content and format issues.

School library RIS encounters a raft of legal and ethical issues. Chapter 9 discusses these issues and suggests ways that school librarians can model and teach ethical information behavior.

RIS is only as effective as its management, providing the conditions for optimum programs. The final chapter covers RIS management issues and strategic planning.

MY INFORMATION EXPERIENCES

As early as age six, when I would ask questions at dinner, my mother would ask me to bring the encyclopedia to the table and share the answer. No wonder my original library career objective was to be a research librarian. I love "looking up things" and helping other people find what they need. I loved working at the reference desk in public and academic libraries. I loved showing students "neat" reference sources and seeing their smiles when they found the article they wanted. And I love teaching pre-service teacher librarians how to polish their research skills, then hear their passion to guide students to be information-literate and good digital citizens. This book builds on my experience and research in reference and information services and offers this knowledge with you—the growing RIS provider.

Chapter One

What Does Reference and Information Service in Today's School Look Like?

Today's world is sometimes known as the Information Society or the Knowledge Society. Even though information swarms around everyone, it can be hard to access, comprehend, and evaluate. In addition, people want and need to find information for workplace, academic, and personal reasons. Even if libraries didn't exist, they would need to be invented in order to fulfill information needs efficiently. This first chapter explores information and its world, information seekers, and the role of school librarians in that world to provide reference and information services.

TODAY'S WORLD

Today's students are growing up in a complex world filled with information and daunting decisions to make. A few statistics make this picture clear.

- Over two million books are published yearly (UNESCO, 2012).
- In 2012 the Internet traffic volume was estimated to be 33.4 exbytes per month and forecast to grow 45 percent to 118 exabytes per month (IBISWorld, 2012).
- In 2011 about 2.5 million people were employed in the information business sector (Bureau of Labor Statistics, 2013).
- One-third of the world's population uses the Internet; more than one billion of these users live in Asia (Miniwatts Marketing Group, 2013).
- Only 5 percent of teens do not access the Internet, and three-quarters have mobile access to the Interent (Duggan & Brenner, 2013).

- Almost three-quarters of eighteen- to twenty-nine-year-olds say that Internet search engines are fair, unbiased sources (Madden et al., 2013).
- Social media usage is highest among adults eighteen to twenty-nine years old. Nowadays, there is little significant difference of use by educational attainment, household income, or urbanity (Duggan & Brenner, 2013).

Even though most students live in the midst of information, they do not necessarily know how to access it effectively, let alone ascertain its validity and relevance, comprehend it, or act upon it (Agosto, 2011; Gasser et al., 2012). Students still tend to ask a person as their first choice of information-seeking strategy. They tend not to use sophisticated searching strategies online or even use relevant keywords and Boolean operations. Many do not have prior content knowledge to critique what information is retrieved or know what to do with it once they find it. Furthermore, students in the United States do not have equitable physical and intellectual access to information, including access to libraries.

Because youth from birth need to make sense of—and deal with—the information that surrounds them and bombards them daily, students need to begin their preparation at the earliest stages of formal education. As educational institutions, K–12 schools provide students with content-rich curriculum, which they need to understand and apply. In so doing, not only do students need to work with information, but educators need to develop and deliver that curriculum, which involves locating and managing information themselves.

Within that framework, school libraries have as their mission "to ensure that students and staff are effective users of ideas and information; students are empowered to be critical thinkers, enthusiastic readers, skillful researchers, and ethical users of information" (American Association of School Librarians, 2009, p. 1). Reference and information services, sometimes referred to as "reference work," constitute a vital part of that function. As information professionals, school librarians serve as mediators between the school community and their information needs: facilitating its availability by gathering and organizing information (both predictable and "as needed") and bridging those intellectual gaps in information behaviors. While the main information issues that school librarians address are academic, both personal and social information can be met with the assistance of school librarians.

INVENTING REFERENCE AND INFORMATION SERVICES

What if reference and information services didn't exist? Would they need to be invented? Try this mental exercise.

Think about your everyday life. Write down possible information needs (e.g., Where can I find a gas station? Why am I having stomach pains? I want to learn Japanese. How do I remove coffee stains? What can I do to stop sales phone calls?).

1. Brainstorm possible information that a student might need: how to solve equations, how to double-space a text document, statistical information, facts such chemical formulas or Cabinet members, why seasons exist, when nuclear energy can be safe, reason for religion.
2. Imagine that libraries and librarians don't exist. How do you find information? Where do you go?
3. Whom do you ask? Whom do you trust?
4. How do you evaluate the information you find?
5. Assume you have very little money. You have no Internet access. You cannot afford to buy books or other information resources. What do you do?
6. What if you want to learn how to be more self-sufficient or more effective in meeting your information needs? How would you go about it? Whom would you ask?
7. What conditions would optimize meeting your information needs? Somewhere along the way, you probably would like to have credible information conveniently located and free to use. You probably would like to contact a dependable, easily available set of people to help you with your information need.
8. In the end, the answer to your information needs might not be the Internet, largely because it is so hard to sort out all the results and determine the quality of information. Most online experts have narrow specializations.
9. In most cases, the best "bang for your buck" is probably the library, and the school librarian is the most likely person to help you become an information expert for yourself.

DEFINING TERMS

Information can vary from a single fact to a broad academic domain of knowledge. Sometimes the general notion of information may be parsed into:

- data: symbols, signs, signals, "raw facts," such as "0" or an arrow
- information: meaningful, functional, organized, or structured data, such as $1+2=3$

- knowledge: information connected in relationship, accumulated synthesis of multiple sources of information over time, such as the ability to explain, calculate, and apply mathematical functions to solve problems.

The source of information is ultimately the creator of information; humans are the de facto originators. For instance, Einstein is generally considered the originator of the general theory of relativity. Humans represent information in words, numbers, images, print artifacts, videos, games, audio files, sculptures, and so on. Continuing the example, Einstein represented the general theory of relativity in the form of equations and an explanatory book. Information resources, therefore, may be considered as information that is recorded (made more or less permanent) in "containers." Libraries focus on *recorded* information, and school libraries focus on recorded information that supports the curriculum and the broader conditions that support student success (which can address personal issues).

Reference resources can be considered any resources that are used to answer an information need. However, the general notion of reference resources tends to think of "ready reference," that is, those materials that contain, and are arranged to locate quickly, specific facts. Such resources are intended for consultation and referral rather than for continuous reading. They are also intended for frequent use, often across curricula, and may be costly. Encyclopedias exemplify the concept of a reference source, but many subject-specific reference sources exist, such as chemical formula tables, timeline references, and gazetteers (RUSA, 2008).

Likewise, reference services range from looking up a specific fact, such as the highest mountain, to providing dissertation research consultation and can vary from a single individual transaction to a self-contained graduate course. The underlying function, in any case, is intellectual access to information. In the strictest definition of a reference transaction, the librarian uses information resources to help people meet their information needs (RUSA, 2000). More broadly, then, reference work encompasses reference transactions as well as other activities that "involve the creation, management, and assessment of information or research resources, tools, and services" (RUSA, 2000, p. 1).

Information services in libraries encompasses even more forms: reader's advisory and other information assistance, signs and other dissemination of information, and the more general concept of access to information, both physical and intellectual (RUSA, 2000). Think of all the information services that the school library provides daily: helping a child find a "fun poem to recite," labelling shelves, finding a review of *Grapes of Wrath* the year that the book was published, collaborating with a teacher on developing a lesson using atlases, researching evidence-based practice on whole language approach to reading, suggesting a novel to help a teen deal with a friend's suicide, developing a list of CAD software to teach architecture, showing how to use the library catalog, creating social bookmarks of websites for third graders on China, publicizing the newest Caldecott Award winner, conducting a workshop for parents on choosing magazines for their children, referring a high school junior to the college counselor. In short, reference and information services constitute a vital part of the total library program. In particular, school librarians must facilitate the physical and intellectual access to a wide variety of information resources that support the curriculum and meet individual needs of the school community.

As exemplified above, school libraries provide physical access to information resources through the organization of the library facility itself, classification schemes, the library catalog, the library web portal, webliographies, directional signs and posters, magazine racks, book displays, reserve shelves, directories, files, Internet-connected computers, other equipment such as televisions and audio players, and assistive technologies.

Intellectual access includes teaching students and staff how to gain competence in information literacy: the ability to locate, select, evaluate, share, manage, use, communicate, and generate information. Again, the options are many and diverse: showing how to use encyclopedia indexes, providing thematic pathfinder research guides, creating screen-capture videos to demonstrate how to find a magazine article in a database, conducting a webinar on copyright fair use, developing customized searching engines, acquiring bilingual dictionaries, coaching teachers on creating online timelines, co-teaching how to take Cornell notes, providing citation style links on the library web portal, demonstrating how to use advanced searching options such as reading level filters, collaboratively designing instruction in web evaluation.

Ideally, all teachers have the same purpose in helping students become effective information users, but each of them has a specific "lens" in this regard. For instance, elementary-grade schoolteachers tend to frame curriculum in terms of age-appropriate content and interaction, in contrast to secondary-grade teachers who use an academic domain as their lodestone so that their students learn how to "think like a mathematician," for instance. Information literacy spans age and curricula at the same time that instruction in intellectual access is particularized for the information task. In that respect, school librarians are most effective when they collaborate with classroom teachers because they can bridge courses across the curriculum and between grades, making for an articulated approach to information literacy and general lifelong learning.

REFERENCE AND INFORMATION SERVICES WITHIN THE SCHOOL LIBRARY PROGRAM

To some extent, the school library program as a whole might be conceptualized as reference and information services. Theoretically, the entire collection exists to meet information needs, and library services seek to help users physically and intellectually access the collection. The American Association of School Librarians' (AASL) 2009 guidelines for school library programs affirm the central role of reference and information services.

- Teaching for learning addresses multiple literacies and emphasizes inquiry-based learning, which depends on information literacy. Effective teaching also involves collaboration, which optimizes information literacy instruction.
- The learning environment focuses on collection and information access, which includes reference sources. It also involves policies, which underscore reference access and use, such as operating hours and circulation practices.
- Leadership can advance the explicit and systematic incorporation of reference and information services into the curriculum.

Again, focusing on the core concepts of reference and information services, the school librarian's reference work may be parsed into resources, access, use, and instruction.

Resources

- Needs assessment: Who is the school community? What is the school's program?
- Collection assessment: What does the library have—and not have? What is its quality?
- Selection: What should be added?
- Acquisition: How will materials be added?
- Presentation: How will materials be processed, organized, and promoted?

Access

- Hours of service: before, during, after school
- Equipment for accessing reference resources
- Group and individual spaces
- Reserve materials on assigned shelves and carts
- Mobile services (i.e., to classes)
- 24-7 access through website

Use

- Use reference sources (productivity)
- Provide information from reference sources
- Teach reference use

Reference Instruction

- Just-in-time interaction: reference transactions, coaching, in-depth consultations
- Planned orientation, independent instruction, collaborative lesson planning
- Products: search aids, bibliographies/pathfinders, online tutorials, websites
- Communication: displays, newsletters, presentations, screencasts

The rest of the book details these aspects of RIS and provides guidance on carrying out these functions effectively to support the information needs of the school community.

GATHERING RIS BASELINE DATA

In order to provide high-quality RIS, baseline data must be collected and analyzed. It is also useful to see good RIS models in action. Assess the current reference services of your library and another strong school library with a school librarian. In investigating RIS, consider the following questions.

Physical Access

- How is reference arranged?
- What provisions are made to meet the needs of diverse populations (e.g., language, physical differences)?
- How is reference indicated (labels, signage, cards, circulation material type, etc.)?
- Describe circulation policy of reference collection (to faculty, students, class, etc.; time period, etc.).
- What is the extent of access to resources (library, from the classroom, remote)?

Intellectual Access

- Describe references instruction (classes, consultation, etc.).
- Describe reference assistance (searches, bookmarking, etc.).
- Describe reference products (guidesheets, bibliographies, Web pages, etc.).
- Describe reference public relations (newsletters, displays, presentations, etc.).
- What is the extent of service by telecommunications?

Planning

Locate possible site/district RIS plans, policies, and procedures.

Compare these data with other local libraries. What are the gaps? What aspects are under your control? What are a couple of action items you can do to improve RIS? The rest of the volume details different aspects of RIS and provides beneficial practices.

REFERENCES

Agosto, D. (2011). Young adults' information behavior: What we know so far and where we need to go from here. *Journal of Research on Libraries and Young Adults, 2*(1). http://www.yalsa.ala.org/jrlya/2011/11/young-adults%E2%80%99-information-behavior-what-we-know-so-far-and-where-we-need-to-go-from-here/.

American Association of School Librarians. (2009). *Empowering learners: Guidelines for school library programs*. Chicago: American Library Association.

Bureau of Labor Statistics. (2013). *Media and information*. Washington, DC: United States Department of Labor.

Duggan, M., & Brenner, J. (2013). *The demographics of social media users*. Washington, DC: Pew Research Center.

Gasser, U., Cortesi, S., Malik, M., & Lee, A. (2012). *Youth and digital media: From credibility to information quality*. Cambridge, MA: Berkman Center for Internet & Society.

IBISWorld. (2012). *Internet traffic volume*. Wilmette, IL: IBISWorld.

Madden, M., Lenhart, A., Duggan, M., Cortesi, S., & Gasser, U. (2013). *Teens and technology 2013*. Washington, DC: Pew Research Center.

Miniwatts Marketing Group. (2013). *Internet world stats*. Bogota, Colombia: Miniwatts Marketing Group.

Reference and User Services Association. (2008). *Definitions of reference*. Chicago: American Library Association.

———. (2000). *Guidelines for information services*. Chicago: American Library Association.

UNESCO Institute of Statistics. (2012). Paris, France: UNESCO.

Chapter Two

Determing Your Community's Needs

In order to provide effective reference and information services (RIS), school librarians need to conduct a thorough needs assessment of the school community and the community at large, as well as the school library's resources and services. This chapter explains how to conduct a needs assessment that includes an environmental scan, in order to collect and analyze data and to determine what services can be provided with existing resources. The assessment can also determine what RIS services might be publicized more or what resources or services could be added or redirected.

ENVIRONMENTAL SCAN

For school library reference and information services to be effective, they have to respond to the information needs of the school community. A needs assessment offers a systematic way to examine the library in the context of the school community and the community at large so school librarians can identify and deliver optimal reference products and information services. This process also results in improving the library program as a whole and increasing its value . In this point in time, school community members have so many information choices that they may be unaware of potentially well-matched options. Especially as the role of the school library is sometimes unclear, school librarians need to define their informational value. In so doing, they should examine their potential user populations. In addition, as the local school site, education in general, and these user populations change, the library program needs to respond in a timely manner in order to stay relevant.

USER POPULATIONS

In order for school library programs to add information value to their user populations, school librarians first need to identify their user populations: their market. The primary user population, which is internal, is the school community, which may be subdivided into students, teachers, support specialists (e.g., nurses, reading coaches), support staff, administrators, and parents. These subdivisions can be further segmented: kindergartners, science teachers, club advisors, and so on. Secondary user populations can include schools in the same or neighboring districts, local libraries and librarians, and the local community at large (including daycare centers, postsecondary institutions, recreation centers, local agencies, bookstores, media outlets, and other businesses). Intervening user populations, those entities that can help send a message to another user population, should also be identified; typical members of that user population include administrators, parents, other librarians, and newspapers. It should be noted that in today's digital society, anyone using social media can assume that role, including students. According to public relations experts Guth and Marsh (2012), for each user population or market segment, school librarians need to know:

- how each influences the library program's ability to provide effective RIS;
- what is its opinion of the library's RIS;
- what its stake or value is relative to the library's RIS;
- who are its opinion leaders and decision makers;
- what are its demographics;
- what are its psychographics (e.g., political leanings, religion, attitudes, values).

Information about the library's user populations can be gathered in many ways: observation, interviews, focus groups, surveys and questionnaires, content analysis of curriculum and student work, school publications, community publications, and even census records.

Developmental Issues

In order to provide effective RIS, school librarians need to know their student populations. Beyond personal interests and academic needs, students are growing developmentally. Those developmental milestones help guide school librarians in providing the reference resources and information services that can be understood and acted upon appropriately.

Primary Grades

- Physical: Some trouble with fine motor and eye-hand coordination, learns kinesthetically, extremely active for short spurts of time, bone growth not complete
- Intellectual: Thinks concretely and literally, learns through repetition, may overgeneralize language rules (e.g., all plurals add an "s"), is learning how to sequence, may confuse fantasy and reality, may have difficulty with concepts of time, is learning that their thoughts differ from others
- Emotional: Wants individual attention and praise, is sensitive about criticism, is curious, expresses emotions freely, realizes their action impact others
- Social: likes social play, is learning to cooperate, needs support and guidance, depends on family, helps others, has a couple of short-term best friends
- Implications for RIS: focus on effort more than results, teach skills that include one to two steps, introduce library and literacy vocabulary, use picture books and stories as ways to learn how to sequence, have students act out directions, teach through simple games, provide multiple opportunities to practice skills (in short spurts)

Upper Elementary Grades

- Physical: high level of energy, has longer mental attention span, gender differences in motor skills
- Intellectual: is gaining technology skills, learns from observation, enjoys reading, skills-oriented, can solve problems, can be persistent, performs well on simple memory tasks, can think logically but may be inconsistent
- Emotional: self-confident and self-aware, is learning to judge situations and consequences, is learning empathy and fairness
- Social: needs supportive reinforcement from family and friends, develops close friendships, belongs to peer groups, makes choices independently of adults, diffentiates between sexes, friends are often same-sex
- Implications for RIS: teach library vocabulary, build on interest in facts, teach skills such as reference tool use, teach research skills structure, incorporate single-sex pairing in activities, incorporate collaboration and competition, teach for mastery, use multimedia resources and information that provides visual cues to text

Middle School

- Physical: rapid physical changes (girls develop earlier than boys generally), may feel awkward, needs physical activity

- Intellectual: benefits from journaling and metacognitive activities, is learning to think abstractly, enjoys word play, likes to develop talents and creativity, curious about the world, may have difficulty with why questions, needs supportive and intellectually stimulating learning environment
- Emotional: experiences emotional changes and mood swings, self-conscious and self-centered, starts to challenge authority, enjoys competition, feels need for fairness and justice, may see world as black-and-white, idealistic, needs privacy
- Social: feels need to conform, peer approval is more important than adult approval, enjoys social media, curious about sex, likes fads
- Implications for RIS: focus on project-based learning, teach research processes, explicitly teach organization and metacognitive skills, encourage self-initiated questions and queries, use technology to reduce egocentrism (e.g., wikis, epals, webinars, virtual field trips), teach point-of-view and incorporate primary sources, teach digital citizenship——and have students create products for peers and children

Mid-Adolescence

- Physical: may be physically and sexually mature, swings between great physical activity and lethargy
- Intellectual: is developing formal logic and moral system, tests new ideas and adult values
- Emotional: needs to experiment and take risks, may be hyper-critical and moody, is starting to explore career goals, growing sense of responsibility and independence
- Social: parents have long-term influence, peers have short-term influence, girls may have anxiety about friendship, may be sexually active, wants to make a difference but may have short-term commitment
- Implications for RIS: incorporate affective domain in learning activities, incorporate dialogue, provide opportunities for short-term civic activities and research, incorporate career exploration activities

Late Adolescence

- Physical: physically and sexually mature
- Intellectual: prepares for the future, thinks abstractly
- Emotional: develops personal identity, integrates moral development and personal moral system, may have emotional disorders (e.g., depression), increased responsibility and independence but still needs adult reinforcement
- Social: has mature interpersonal and likely sexual relationships

- Implications for RIS: provide post-secondary reference resources, incorporate life skills in information-seeking processes, provide local referral sources, teach how to use specialized reference tools, collaborate with teachers to help students conduct domain-specific research (e.g., think like a scientist), provide opportunities for civic understanding and participation, encourage building positive digital reputations, offer library aide training and projects

Special Populations

Even within each population clustered by function or age, several subgroups have unique needs that deserve specific consideration.

Immigrants constitute about 10 percent of the U.S. population. Even with globalization, these newcomers may be unaware of educational and social practices, and they may face prejudice as well as language barriers. Newcomers are more likely to be poor than the average U.S. citizen and may feel isolated as they experience culture shock. Library services in their original country probably differ significantly from U.S. services, particularly for school libraries. Even in those U.S. schools where the library is managed by a paraprofessional, that person is probably more educated and trained than in most other countries, and the collections are very likely to be richer and more current. Furthermore, materials are usually available in several formats, and technology that students may access is usually more extensive in the United States. In many countries, the library stacks are closed, and students might have to rent materials rather than borrow them freely. U.S. library services are also likely to be more extensive, especially in terms of RIS. School librarians should make a special effort to identify recent immigrants and give them a customized orientation. In the process, students can share their prior library experiences, which can inform library staff about differences in resources and services.

Both immigrants and U.S. residents might be non-English speakers. In addition, English language learners may constitute a significant percentage of the school population. U.S. school libraries tend to focus on English reference sources, though they may include materials used in world language courses. Students who read in non-Roman language systems face additional barriers in using keyboards (although even other Roman-alphabet languages may have a slightly different keyboard arrangement). Fortunately, digital reference sources are increasingly available in non-English languages, particularly Spanish, and formats often enable one to copy-paste into online translation tools such as Google's product or those listed at http://libguides. library.albany.edu/content.php?pid=57538&sid=433044. Over the years, these translation applications have improved because users have provided recommended translation specifics, and the number of languages supported by translation programs has also increased. For short passages, students might also consider using the free app Word Lens, which visually scans a page and translates it on the fly. They can also pick up visual cues. In some cases, students can understand spoken English better than written language, so they can use text-to-speech features, which are available on PC and Mac operating systems, as well as more sophisticated software programs such as Jaws, which was originally developed for people with visual impairments. In addition, librarians can provide an international (or at least non-English) webpage on their library portal that links to educational non-English reference directories (e.g., http://www.dmoz.org/Reference/ and http://www.lib. berkeley.edu/doemoff/govinfo/intl/gov_eu.html) and search engines (e.g., http://www.searchenginesindex.com/ and http://www.searchenginecolossus. com/). Even Wikipedia in non-English languages can serve as a starting point, and Wikipedia is also available in simple English (http://simple. wikipedia.org/). Similarly to English language learners, illiterate and aliterate students can use technology to read text aloud, depend on visual cues, and use video reference sources.

Students with disabilities, be they chronic or temporary, constitute approximately 20 percent of the population. The Individuals with Disabilities Education Act identifies fourteen types of disabilities, which include different sensate and physical impairments, learning disabilities, emotional disturbances, communication disorders, and other health issues. These students face a variety of access and processing issues as they seek information. They may have physical limitations that make it harder to engage with the material, or they may have internal processing differences, such as dyslexia or neural disorders, that cause difficulties in comprehending the information. Some may have problems asking for help because of language or social interaction challenges. At the same time, they may feel isolated or need to depend on others in order to achieve. Their information needs echo the needs of their typical peers—academics, personal interests and issues—and they also want specific information that addresses their unique disabilities, showing them ways to succeed. Librarians need to match resources and services to specific needs, while aiming for inclusivity. For instance, instruction should provide clear, simple step-by-step directions and routines, combined with visual scaffolding. The library itself needs to optimize physical access through reachable shelving, adaptable computers, appropriate assistive technology, and open traffic areas.

Adult Needs

The school community includes a wide variety of support personnel and families, each of whom has distinct information needs associated with work or personal life. Classroom teachers generally need subject-specific or pedagogical resources, with an eye on proven practices. Administrators welcome data-based research on school issues, including legal information. Service personnel may need help locating supportive resources to help their clientele, such as non-English health websites. Cocurricular advisors and coordinators may want specialized resources such as sports rules or local business contacts. Families may appreciate parenting reference materials and local community service information. School personnel information needs are likely to change over the years as they become more expert in their work or face different challenges in their personal life journeys.

It should be noted that immigrant and English learner youth may well have to serve as translators and information mediators for their families. Thus, they may ask about available social services or inquire about health issues of older adults. Such information seeking can be particularly daunting for these students, who have no concept of welfare services or menopause. Usually school librarians refer these questions to public librarians, or they can work with the school's parent teacher organization to provide information sessions for immigrant or non-English-speaking families with guest speakers from public agencies.

SWOT ANALYSIS

To meet users' needs, school librarians need to identify what they can offer in terms of products and services: the internal environment. They also need to analyze the context or external environment to understand the issues that impact their user populations—and the library's own ability to provide needed resources and services. The term "external" may be applied to the school, the school district, the local community, the larger geographic region, or another outside entity.

One foundation for market and community analysis is a SWOT analysis (strength, weakness, opportunity, threat). In school libraries, internal strengths and weaknesses may arise from personnel, boards, support groups, facilities, money, collections, services, technology, curriculum, instruction, library portals and other access guides, operating hours, and so on. External factors might be school and community demographics, curriculum and co-curriculum, standards, library and school competitors, technology, politics, governments at different levels, public and private agencies, economic environment, legal environment, and so forth.

A SWOT analysis can be based on the total library program, or it can focus on one or two aspects of the program. Since one of the functions of the school library is RIS instruction, a focused SWOT analysis might identify:

- current RIS curriculum that is provided in the school library and offered by competitors such as classroom teachers, public libraries, and online information providers;
- existing and potential instructors and instructional designers in the school library and elsewhere;
- existing and potential RIS resources, including learning aids, in the school library and elsewhere;
- existing and potential learners *and* learning needs, in the school library and elsewhere.

School librarians do well to align efforts with schoolwide priorities. In that respect, SWOT analysis can help clarify a compelling situation in terms of the RIS role that that library can play. For instance, students might be performing poorly on standardized tests (certainly a significant concern for the school community). Alternatively, a growing incidence of cyberbullying might be negatively impacting the school. A SWOT analysis might uncover the following factors for the second situation:

- Strengths: rich digital collection that supports the curriculum, class set of Internet-connected computers, access throughout the day, flexible scheduling, tech-savvy library staff, filtering software used, acceptable use policy (AUP) in place, good relations with the public library
- Weaknesses: no library lessons on cyberbullying, no mention of cyberbullying or digital safety beyond AUP on library website, no information on local community hotlines
- Opportunities: e-rate compliance requires instruction on digital safety, administrators and teachers don't know how to deal with cyberbullying (school librarian can serve as an expert)
- Threats: no place in the curriculum for digital safety instruction, administrators and parents want to cut off access to all social media, technicians don't want to deal with intranets or social media.

Once school librarians know what RIS they can offer—or have the capacity to provide—they can determine which market to target. If school librarians try to reach everyone, that approach is called mass marketing and tries to find an issue or value that is the common denominator for everyone. Alternatively, school librarians can focus on a few key market segments to provide more specific services or approaches. In general, school librarians tend to segment markets (that is, potential users) by age or type of use: for example, parents who want to volunteer in the library, reluctant readers, techies, manga fans. Typically, an organization has resources or services that are underused or undervalued that they want to push. Perhaps they see a target user market potential that has ignored them. In general, school librarians should try to go to the biggest bang for the buck: the best return for their efforts. For instance, a likely niche is entering users: new students and employees. Referring to the SWOT example above, school librarians might target health classes.

At this point, school librarians can gather more specific data that can inform their marketing decisions. A needs assessment is an effective way to find out about the current knowledge, capabilities, interests, and values of each school community segment. Following the above example, through a schoolwide survey, the school librarian may find out that few people understand cyberbullying legalities or where to get help. On the other hand, the school librarian may discover that 97 percent of students use social media and 36 percent have been involved in cyberbullying. The school librarian should also assess the learning context. How might cyberbullying fit into the curriculum? How might the school schedule fit into cyberbullying RIS?

THINK GLOBALLY; ACT LOCALLY

As school librarians "scope the scene," they should consider international implications. As noted above, the school community could well include new immigrants, as well as natives who speak other languages or have ties to other countries. The curriculum certainly has international subject matter, and greater numbers of schools are adopting international baccalaurete standards, which seek to develop intercultural understanding and world improvement through international education. Technology has greatly expanded access to resources throughout the world. Globalization is now an economic fact, with the awareness that the world is interdependent. Today's students must prepare to be global citizens.

Thus, when conducting a SWOT analysis, school librarians should consider using a global "lens" or perspective.

- What do today's students—and the school community at large— need to know and do in order to thrive in a global society?
- What information needs do they have that could be addressed through internationally enriched library RIS?
- What international reference sources do they need to access and use?
- What reference and information services could be improved through the use of international experts?
- How might the school community benefit from connections with school library RIS in other countries?

Fortunately, several professional library associations have international elements that can help school librarians serve as globally aware RIS providers.

- The American Library Association (ALA) has a strong Canadian presence, as well as other international members. The association itself has several committees and offices that provide international resources: International Relations Round Table (http://www.ala.org/ irrt/), International Relations Office (http://www.ala.org/offices/iro), and international advocacy (http://www.ala.org/advocacy/ international). In 2012 the Association of College and Research Libraries developed standards for cultural competencies for academic libraries (http://www.ala.org/acrl/standards/diversity), which are very relevant for school librarians.
- The International Federation of Library Associations and Institutions (IFLA) has a School Libraries section (http://www.ifla.org/school-libraries-resource-centers) and several groups that address issues internationally, such as information literacy, information technology, literacy and reading, collection development, and training, as well as reference and information services.
- The International Association of School Librarianship (http://www. iasl-online.org) addresses the needs of school librarians around the world and is particularly useful at the site level for peer collaboration around the world.

CONCLUSIONS

Conducting a needs assessment provides a systematic way for school librarians to both satisfy their user populations and improve RIS and the library program as a whole. To that end, the school library needs assessment encompasses both internal practices and collaboration with several user populations. The above SWOT analysis reveals a great opportunity for school librarians to provide new value to library RIS. In the above example, a school community goal could be a reduction in student cyberbullying, with the library program playing a key role in reaching that goal. The specific objective would follow: to provide reference and information services to the school community about cyberbullying and how to deal with it. As resource and information processing experts, school librarians are uniquely positioned to document, communicate about, and assess RIS efforts. Concurrently, assessing each step can ensure that ensuing planning and implementation are done effectively, the bottom line being value-added, improved school library RIS.

REFERENCE

Guth, D., & Marsh, C. (2012). *Public relations: A values-driven approach* (5th ed.). Boston: Allyn & Bacon.

Chapter Three

Assessing Information Behaviors

Part of the needs assessment should address information behaviors of the school community—and library staff. Indeed, in order for school librarians to provide effective reference and information service, they need to build a wide repertoire of information-seeking strategies themselves. This chapter discusses different information behaviors, drawing upon current theories. Next, the chapter provides techniques for effectively researching and retrieving information from different types of print, nonprint, and digital resources. In the process, techniques for searching visual and aural information are also provided.

INTERACTING WITH INFORMATION

At the most basic level, information literacy deals with human interaction with information in its various forms. This interaction is ultimately between two people, usually through the intermediary of recorded expression of a person's ideas. In that respect, the interaction is often an unclosed communication loop in that the receiver of the information might not be able to respond to the message sender such that the originator will get feedback.

Even before the interaction, both the person and the information preexist and are situationally contextualized, even if the information is not recorded. In most cases, the information provider wants to influence others, be it an artist or an politician. The other party might be actively seeking information or not.

At the first interactive stage, awareness, a person becomes aware of either some piece of information (a stimulus) or the need for information to solve a problem. For instance, a person may see a stop sign or is lost and needs directions. One approach is other-initiated or reactive (becoming aware of

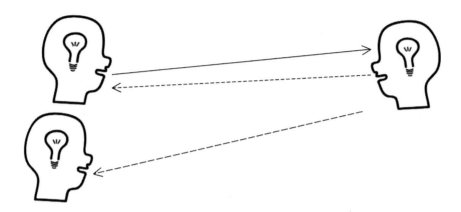

Figure 3.1.   Communication model.

information), and the other approach is self-initiated or proactive (seeking information).

Even in this initial stage, a person makes a decision: whether to ignore the information—or information need—or to engage with it. For instance, a person may see a magazine but not be interested in looking at it. Similarly, a person might hear a radio advertisement that he already knows and stops listening to it.

If the person decides to engage with the information, then several actions occur. The person tries to comprehend the information. That task involves decoding (e.g., visuals, sound, linguistic language) and understanding the content (e.g., vocabulary, semiotics, concepts). Each format has its unique features, such as layout protocols (e.g., a newspaper layout differs from a magazine or a book), image "grammar" (e.g., use of color, shape, composition), and sound effects; if the person doesn't understand how a format "works," misunderstanding of the content may result.

Next the person evaluates that information: what impact does the information have upon the person? If the information reinforces the person's current knowledge base, then learning does not occur. If the information adds to the knowledge base, then learning can occur. If, however, the information contradicts the current knowledge base (e.g., evolution versus creationism), then the person has to decide how to reconcile the opposing information or to reject one piece. If the new piece of information is accepted, then learning occurs. If should be noted that the evaluative selection or rejection of information can involve cognitive, affective, and behavioral factors. For example, if someone says that smoking is unhealthy, a person might reject that statement because the pleasure involved in smoking might overshadow scientific evidence. Evaluation also takes into account the information task at hand:

how the information is to be used. For instance, even if smoking is unhealthy, a person might be studying how tobacco grows and not care about its impact on human lungs. It should also be noted that at this point, engagement with the information can stop.

Evaluation has more of a consumer mind-set in that the person is receiving the information. When that person continues to engage with the information, starting to manipulate it, then the mind-set resembles that of a producer. The individual uses the information as a basis for change. Several actions are possible: interpretation, organization, synthesis, reformatting, translating, changing, relating, or combining with other information. Again, such manipulation is usually associated with an explicit information task. In the case where a person is reacting to an information stimulus, such as stop sign, the person may see a need to act upon that information. Even if a person sees a deer and decides to ignore it, if the deer hits the car, then an information task will ensue: how to repair the car.

A person can manipulate information and not act upon it or apply it; the engagement can stop at that point. For instance, a person might translate a poem but not write down the translation or otherwise communicate it. On the other hand, a person is probably more likely to manipulate information because he or she has a task with a goal in mind, such as having a car that operates properly (which was problematic due to the deer who hit it, for example). The goal might be as straightforward as needing to write a five-page report on how tobacco grows as a class assignment (the longer-term goal being to earn an A in biology, which might lead to acceptance into medical school, and so on). As these examples illustrate, goals differ in terms of time frame as well as context: for example, solving a problem, self-improvement, contribution to society's knowledge base. Even after applying the information, a person might continue to engage with that information by linking it to a new context or information task. Likewise, even when a person is finished engaging with the information, the information need might still remain, at which point the person has to decide whether to engage with more information or not.

At each step above, a person can decide to disengage. For instance, when the information need is satisfied, no further engagement may be warranted. The information—or its need—has to be motivating enough to keep one involved. Moreover, the effort has to be worth any obstacles encountered, such as physical or intellectual access issues, socioeconomic parameters, legalities, or procedural issues. Furthermore, one's own psychological make-up can impact the degree and depth of engagement; if a person is easily frustrated or has few coping strategies, then he or she might give up, while another person with greater resiliency and sense of persistence is more likely to persevere.

The Added Task of Information Seeking

Information seeking represents an additional, self-initiated step in information behavior beyond engagement. In order to seek (and find) information, a person has to: (1) identify an issue, even if it is just a self-awareness that something is "off"; (2) realize that information is needed; (3) determine the information gap, that is, what information exists and what information is needed; (4) decide to seek information. These steps occur within the context of the person and his or her situational environmental. Furthermore, these steps all occur before the actual action of locating information, and they are revisited after locating the information to verify that the search has been accomplished or to readjust the task.

The actual step of locating the information involves: (1) identifying the the domain or "universe" in which information may be located (e.g., family members, the local community's members and agencies, the "free" Internet, subscription databases); (2) determining possible seeking constraints (e.g., time frame, reading ability, language barriers, transportation, technology and Internet access limitations, money); (3) planning a searching strategy (e.g., types of materials, locational tools such as indexes and catalogs, key terms and questions, sequence of action); (4) implementing the plan. Even when a likely resource is found and evaluated (that is, engaging with the information), the person still has to locate the needed information *within* the selected source, which involves using key terms and locational tools such as tables of contents, indexes, and visual cues (e.g., headings, tables, illustrations).

Once the information is located and retrieved, then the engagement process comes into play. As such, the seeker evaluates the information and determines whether other information is needed. However, it is apparent that the overall set of processes depends on the individual's factors (e.g., language skills, subject matter knowledge, attitudes, etc.), resource variables (e.g., amount and type of information available, access devices, etc.), and contextual variables (e.g., origin of information task or need, conditions of the activity, social environment, etc.) (Lazonder & Rouet, 2008).

As implied above, information engagement involves more than cognitive processes. Carol Kuhlthau (2004) is the best-known researcher in this area. In tracking people's emotional state as they seek and engage with information, she found predictable patterns in that process:

1. First encounter: uncertainty, curiosity, fear of the unknown, hopefulness
2. Selection: increasing focus and optimism
3. Exploration: possible confusion and doubt, especially if information conflicts
4. Formulation: increased clarity and confidence

5. Collection in light of formuation: increased interest and confidence, deeper involvement
6. Presentation: satisfaction or resignation

Between the time that individuals begin engagement and finish, they tend to gain certainty, confidence, satisfaction (or acceptance).

Intermediaries

The above discussion focuses on direct engagement between a person (or group) and information. The concept of intermediary or indirect engagement is not mentioned. Nevertheless, the most common source of information is another person, typically one who is known, trusted, and considered to be an expert. In the eyes of a child, that person is usually a parent. When locating a recorded information resource, a person is likely to ask an intermediary for help in locating such a resource: a relative or friend who has had a similar information need, an expert in the area of need (e.g., an algebra teacher or tutor for help in mathematics), or (less frequently) a librarian. Generally, if the intermediary is not known, subject expertise seems to trump general resource expertise (i.e., the librarian), and an individual is preferable to an institution as an information mediary (Abrahamson, Fisher, Turner, Durrance, & Turner, 2008; Harris & Dewdney, 1994). These intermediaries can get involved at any step in the process:

- providing information
- drawing attention to information
- causing the information need
- defining the information task
- helping identify the needed information
- impacting the context of the information need or its locational process
- influencing the searching strategy
- helping provide physical access to the information
- supporting comprehension (e.g., guided reading, translating, contextualization)
- helping evaluate the information (e.g., through instruction, checklists, rubrics)
- helping manipulate the information (e.g., through technical support, instruction, templates)
- helping applying the information (e.g., through communication and implementation venues).

In some cases, the person engaged with the information may ask for mediation, but in other cases, another party may be actively interjecting into the interactivity or merely coincidentally influencing the engagement (such as closing the library when the person wants to access the library collection).

It should also be noted that one information resource can lead to another as authors cite their source materials. In that respect, recorded information itself might be considered as a mediary or access tool. For instance, library catalogs and other bibliographies serve as mediaries. Unfortunately, students do not like using such mediaries, preferring to be able to access information directly (Borgman, Hirsh, & Walter, 1995). For that reason, full-text database aggregators are much more acceptable and useful than citation-only databases, and single-search library catalogs that can retrieve articles as well as full-text e-books are even more popular.

INFORMATION BEHAVIORS

Information behaviors draw upon several theories: cognitivism, behaviorism, and social learning. A newer theory, Radical Change, is rooted in digital age principles of greater interactivity, connectivity, and access, which impact both information and information behaviors (Dresang, 1999). Operationally, differences in information behavior may arise from internal processing differences, maturation, knowledge base, and interaction with external factors (Henry, 2005).

Some information behaviors cross generations; Harris and Dewdney (1994) identified several principles of information-seeking behaviors that continue to resonate. Information needs are situational, and the decision to seek help is impacted by many factors. In general, people try to find answers to the information quickly with the least effort, and they tend to ask another person first before looking at a material resource. In rank order, information seekers select to ask: (1) people of convenience, (2) friends or peers with comparable experience, and (3) experts. Sadly, students tend to consider teachers and librarians as negative social types (Shenton & Dixon, 2004); in specific, the school library may be perceived as having only curricular information, not anything that might address personal interests and needs (Todd, 2003). In addition, when people are consulted, the seeker expects emotional support. Information seekers also tend to use the same resources if they have retrieved satisfactory results in the past, building on success. Well-known resources, be they *World Book* or Wikipedia or popular search engines such as Google, are often first choices too. Convenient, "good enough" information is usually preferred to the best information if the latter takes too much time and effort to obtain (Purcell et al., 2012). Of course, the value of the information impacts that decision; for instance, if a person has unlimited resources, he or she would probably look for the best cancer surgeon for a loved one rather than a "good enough" physician. Likewise, if the person just wants to confirm his or her existing beliefs, then "just enough" information is needed for affirmation; conflicting information would likely be avoided.

Nevertheless, age accounts for much of the differences in information behaviors, just as information needs reflect age-dependent academic and personal concerns. For instance, mental processing is impacted by brain development, and physical development affects kinesthetic skills. Effective information seeking requires higher cognitive and metacognitive skills, which harkens back to Piaget's stages of development. Personal and familial background and experiences impact the development of knowledge structures and interactions with one's environment. Lu (2010) also noted that children develop a sense of control as they mature and are more likely to seek information if they think that they have some power to control the situation; children are also more likely to think that the information found is more useful if the information need is in their control.

Children's Information Behaviors

Youngsters' personal information needs are usually handled by adults in the immediate family. Therefore, most of the literature about children's information behaviors focuses on school work. Information tasks are usually defined—and imposed—by the teacher; when their students do not understand the reason for the task, or do not have the background knowledge to engage with the information knowingly, they miss key concepts (Gross, 1999; Nesset, 2013). Furthermore, their limited knowledge base limits their ability to evaluate information critically; indeed, most youngsters do not question the authority of the sources (Lubans, 1999). Nevertheless, children do seek information to cope with their own day-to-day and personal problems, either to solve or escape their problems (Lu, 2010).

In terms of choosing resources, children prefer to browse within a narrow range of shelves where they have successfully found information in the past (Borgman, Hirsh, & Walter, 1995). However, with the growing presence of the Internet, even young students tend to prefer online information to print resources (Large et al., 2008). As noted above, children prefer not to use any intermediary tools and often have difficulty navigating online library catalogs (Borgman, Hirsh, & Walter, 1995; Large et al., 2008). Even though Google is not geared to young readers, children overwhelming choose this search engine as their primary method of seeking recorded information, to a large part because the results are often immediately accessible without having to go elsewhere; in fact, some student equate "googling" with researching (Bilal, 2012; Purcell et al., 2012). Furthermore, when children use search engines, they tend to choose just the first page of "hits" because they have a hard time determining the relative relevance and quality of those websites. On the other hand, children rate meaningful content as the most important consideration in evaluating a website, followed by engagement, organization, overall impression, and enjoyment factor (Loh & Williams, 2003). Foss et al. (2012) identified seven types of information searching strategies among grade schoolers: developing (limited knowledge of search tools and strategies), domain-specific (a specific topic of interest), power search (leveraging search features), social (use social networking), nonmotivated, rule-bound (using the same strategies all the time), and visual (retrieving visual sources).

Based on these realities, school librarians should focus on concrete information tasks and provide understandable examples. Graphic organizers can help children sequence their actions and structure their work. Concept mapping offers a visual way to organize throughts and can accommodate different ways of thinking, particularly since by the time a child is seven years old, his or her learning style is largely set (Ames, 2003). Because children are building their vocabulary knowledge, librarians should explicitly teach information literacy terms and show students how to find synomyms. Posters of key terms, accompanied by appropriate visual cues, scaffold and reinforce these concepts. Even at this young age, librarians should offer children options in their information tasks, such as choosing between a couple of encyclopedias or websites.

In terms of technology use, most youngsters have explored some type of digital device by the time they enter kindergarten. Nevertheless, their fine motor skills are still developing, so they should have smaller keyboards to fit their hand size. More fundamentally, children's bodies and motor skills need development and coordination; computer use should be brief for little ones in order to prevent obesity and vision problems. Usually a combination of on-computer and off-computer activity within a learning task yields the best academic and social results (American Association for the Advancement of Science, 1999).

Teens' Information Behaviors

What kinds of information are young people seeking? Agosto's 2011 summary of young adults' information needs provides a good starting point for consideration:

- relationships (family, peers, etc.);
- other emotional needs;
- health and safey, including sexuality;
- academics, including college;
- careers/jobs;
- recreational and leisure interests;
- popular culture;
- consumer needs.

Agosto and Hughes-Hassell (2006) emphasized the importance of social factors in youth development and noted that information seeking and use helps teens develop their cognitive, sexual, social, emotional, reflective, physical, and creative selves.

Heinström (2006) identified three types of information search behaviors: surface, deep, and strategic, which were tied to the students' motivation for the particular task at hand. Dresang and Koh (2009) developed a typology of youth information behaviors based on Radical Change theory: changing forms of cognitive aspects, identity and value negotiation, and changing information access and seeking community. In researching teens' use of information about heroin, Todd (2003) identified five types of cognitive information use: "get a complete picture, get a verified picture, get a changed picture, get clearer picture, and get a position in a picture" (pp. 39–40); teens are trying to get information and then form opinions and act.

How do youth satisfy their information wants and needs? Gasser et al. (2012) explored how youth use digital media to seek information. Not surprisingly, more than 90 percent of teens use the Internet. Nevertheless, youth consult a wide variety of sources, including human, to answer their information questions. Their choices of source depend on several factors: purpose, motivation, convenience, time frame, trust, competency and self-efficacy, and demographics.

Overall, youth start where they were successful before, staying within their information literacy comfort zone. Often they are unaware of online subscription article databases because either they have not been given associated instruction—by the school or public librarian—or they do not have access to such databases due to libraries' financial constraints. If they need just a little print information, they are most likely to consult a general encyclopedia by pulling out the likely volume; going first to the index volume is not the usual pattern. If they need more in-depth information, they will typically search the online library catalog for a book on the subject; looking for a chapter within a book is less common—and they may walk away from the catalog if there's not a whole book on their topic (e.g., electrodes) rather than searching under a more general subject heading (e.g., electricity) and then looking in the book's index. As students mature, they seek a wider spectrum of research but may still favor quantity over quality. As a result, they may get information that they cannot comprehend or information that doesn't answer the research question (Savolainen & Kari, 2004; Shenton & Dixon, 2004).

Students' research strategy is goal-centered; the process is not the main focus. The context for the research also might not be important to them. If there's an easy way to get the answer, students gravitate to that approach. Typically using a "convenience" model, teens tend to ask family and friends, check materials at home, download the first Google hit, or consult Wikipedia. In terms of their searching strategy, even teens tend to use unsophisticated methods. Indeed, even the notion of keywords eludes some preteens and teenagers (Branch, 2001). They might not know the term but get the idea if the librarian teacher refers to the use of synonyms. Surprisingly, many teens do not understand—or choose not to use—Boolean operators. In fairness, Boolean AND and OR "behave" differently in formal logic situations than in everyday English. If Joe likes carrots and peas, it means he likes both: together or apart. But if Joe wanted to find out about carrots and about peas, he would need to input "carrots OR peas." Search engines might not provide that option except for advanced searching, which teens do not instantly see and so might ignore. If anything, students are more likely to type in whole phrases in natural language rather than input "staccato"-like terms: "What are the breeding habits of elephants?" rather than "elephant and reproduction." Likewise, students seldom use wildcard characters or make good use of "clustering" phrase symbols such as quotation marks, parentheses, or plus signs. In researching preteen and teen research behaviors, Purcell et al. (2012) interviewed teachers, who asserted that digital search tools have advantaged students, but these tools also contributed to students' "surface" searching and short attention spans.

Context also impacts students as they evaluate the source: what is the perspective, how accurate is it, how thorough is it, how useful is it for the purpose of solving the problem? Students sometimes do not give a critical eye to resources and instead consider any piece of information as "holy script," particularly if it is found online. Students might not consider the perspective of the author or understand the context of the information. For instance, a scientist is likely to have a different perspective than a religious leader when discussing stem-cell research. Fortunately, today's youth are becoming more information savvy. In testing eleven- to seventeen-year-olds' ability to detect good and bad information, Flanagan and Metzger (2010) found that students realize the negative consequences of believing false information, and they pay close attention when the information need is highly valued. Students tend to overestimate their ability to critically and accurately evaluate websites; younger students tend to be less trustful of websites, but older students are more concerned about the quality of information. In another "bright-spot" study, which investigated how youth evaluate information, Gasser et al. (2012) culled the following criteria used: topicality, relevance (that is, match with the intended purpose), utility, significance, credibility, domain name (e.g., edu and gov are preferred to com websites), popularity, amount of information, visual attractiveness, interactivity, peer opinion, and personal preference.

It should be noted that students may follow a very sequential research process whereby the evaluation comes *only* at the end, and revisiting the search question or strategy might not occur to teens. This attitude really undermines teens who are not clear about their original task; they may soon become confused. On one hand, if they are easily frustrated, they may just walk away from the whole project (or borrow other people's work); however, they may doggedly persist in a fruitless direction, seemingly unable to change tactics halfway through. In either case, they are not successful. When such experiences occur last-minute, because the teen did not plan ahead or miscalculated the amount of time needed to conduct the research process, success again evades them.

Here are some of teenagers' RIS truisms, culled from Lien (2000), Lubans (1999), and Vansickle (2002):

- Wikipedia is king.
- Google is awesome.
- Want news? Go online.
- Social networking is good for homework.
- IM is better than e-mail; e-mail is so yesterday—it's for old people and teachers.
- If information isn't on the front page, it probably isn't worthwhile anyway.
- "Good enough" is good enough.
- Free is good.
- Downloading is OK as long as you're not selling it.
- I get scared sometimes, but I can take care of myself.

Meyers, Fisher, and Marcoux (2009) focused on the everyday information behaviors of preteens, which differs somewhat from older teens, particularly in terms of social and emotional factors. Preteens, for instance, need a supportive environment for seeking information; they weigh the emotional and social costs of inquiry and information sharing (for example, possible embarrassment about asking the librarian a question may result in not pursuing the question). Trust is paramount in information seeking. Preteens prefer interpersonal sources and informal social spaces for everyday information rather than formal channels such as schools and libraries.

Agosto (2011) also synthesized researchers' identification of barriers experienced in youths' information behaviors. Some barriers rest with the searcher: lack of subject knowledge, lack of knowledge about how to locate and use source material, discomfort with the information task or the information itself (e.g., not wanting to know about spiders), feeling overwhelmed by information or the task, social discomfort, and negative feelings about libraries or librarians. Other barriers are external to the youth: access barriers and other use restrictions such as library closures, lack of available resources, lack of access to technology, and lack of transportation. Gasser et al. (2012) added the challenges of information complexity and distractions. Still other barriers have been identified: lack of language, literacy, technology, and research skills; as well as lack of motivation and low estimation of an imposed information task (Farmer, 2003).

Within the broad teenage population exists the information poor, who experience even more challenges (Chapman & Pendleton, 1995). They don't think they can help themselves. They behave secretly and deceptively to protect what information they have, and they don't think people outside their class would share information with them. They are unlikely to take social risks, but they may be successful within their own culture. Potentially, their information lives are a closed universe. Technology-based RIS can empower them and help them link with other groups.

When students go on to postsecondary educational settings, they often find that they are not "college-ready" after all. In a study of college freshmen, Oakleaf and Owen (2010) discovered that all of these students had to create an inquiry-based research project and that almost of them interacted with websites and articles. In the process, these first-year students had to construct an effective search strategy and evaluate websites, as well as incorporate and cite the information. Oklahoma State University's library developed a bibliography of resources about preparing students for college research (http://www.library.okstate.edu/cml/hotspot.html). In studying the gap between high school and college information literacy, Schroeder (2009) found that the biggest learning gap for college freshmen was finding information: using the library catalog, understanding the Library of Congress Classification system, knowing how to choose a database, determining the best kinds of sources for the information task, and differentiating among types of resources (e.g., scholarly peer-reviewed journals versus trade magazines, primary sources, empirical research versus commentary). Projectlit.org studied college students' information-seeking behaviors (Head, 2013) and discovered that two-thirds of students stated that defining a topic was the most difficult task, 80 percent didn't ask librarians for help, and over 80 percent used Wikipedia to get background information. In addition, some college freshman are just scared of academic libraries (Bailey, 2008).

Ethical Issues in Teens' Information Behavior

Particularly in terms of responsibility, students' information behavior reflects their developmental issues. As noted in chapter 2, teens have to adjust to major bodily and emotional changes. At the same time, they are encountering more complex situations for which they have to make decisions, such as sexuality and other health issues, recreational options including substance abuse and extreme physical activities, and workplace issues. In response, teens are likely to be impulsive and prone to focus on and overestimate short-term payoffs and underplay longer-term consequences of what they do, and they are likely to overlook alternative courses of action (Winters, 2008). In terms of brain development, teens are forming their formal abstract logic abilities and values system (Dobbs, 2011). Thus, they might not make logical assumptions or think through their decisions to their logical consequences, with the result that they do not pace themselves realistically when conducting research or realize that they may get caught plagiarizing. When those negative consequences occur, teenagers' neural circuits overload, activating swinging emotional moods and spiraling them down further. At the same time, the brain is wired to encourage risk taking, so librarians should leverage this tendency by facilitating intellectual risk taking.

These developments impact technology RIS in particular since teens may know how to do technical tasks such as creating and downloading digital information, but they might still struggle with realizing that they should not take that action (e.g., flaming others, pirating music). Therefore, school librarians need to explicitly teach responsible use, scaffolding teens' moral decision-making processes. On the other hand, technology also helps teens' information behavior. Teens can access relevant resources from around the world and choose materials that fit their learning preferences. In online environments, they are not as prone to peer critiques about their physical differences. Access to 24-7 RIS gives teens more control as they can choose when to ask for help and can "hide" behind the computer interface, thus minimizing feelings of vulnerability. In addition, social media facilitates collaborative learning.

General RIS Implications

The issue of information behavior has direct bearing on reference and information skills. In many cases, students have not had the opportunity to learn and practice these skills. Gasser et al. (2012) also synthesized research in this arena and found that youth learn in personal, social, and academic contexts. For example, youth gain information skills through trial and error when engaging in creative activities, games, and virtual communities. As the main venue for formal education of youth, schools bear the responsibility for teaching students these skills. More specifically, school librarians are the best trained and best positioned professionals to provide this training. It should be noted that such instruction usually is based on adult-normative standards rather than on student-centric information creation, which blends personal and social context.

THEORIES OF INFORMATION BEHAVIOR

Several theories and models try to explain information-seeking behaviors. Here are some representative examples collected by Wilson (2013).

- Activity theory studies how human behavior acts upon objects to transform them. Six principles guide the interaction: the unity of consciousness and activity, object-orientation (be it material or human), internalization of conditions and externalization of processing, mediation by others, and hierarchical structure of activity and development. The person's motive determines the information goal, which is affected by other conditions. The motive generates the activities, which are composed of operational action. This theory is often applied to games and problem solving.
- Personal construct theory, developed by George Kelly in the 1950s, focuses on ways that individuals make meaning of their experiences and organize systems of personal constructs over time. The individual has agency and autonomy, so that information and its use is not a top-down given. This theory influenced Kuhlthau's work in inquiry searching.
- Personality theory focuses on traits that indicate likely behavior patterns, noting that context can influence those behaviors. Core principles include: stability and generality of behavior over time and under different conditions, genetic base for behavior, and interaction patterns. Five core dimensions include: negative emotionality/neuroticism, extroversion, openness to experience, agreeableness, and conscientiousness. Other theories of personality include the psychodynamic view, learning perspectives, humanistic perspective, cognitive perspective, and biological perspective. Personality appears to overshadow subject domain in terms of information-seeking behaviors and influences technology acceptance and use.
- Practice theory deals with skills and knowledge used to perform a concrete practice, building on social values and rules (i.e., social construction and social identity). Process, routine, and change are key concerns. Practice theory applies well to knowledge management, organizational thinking about technology, and social media practice.
- Social cognitive theory, originally called social learning theory, was introduced by Albert Bandura. It started with ideas of imitation theory, included principles of observational learning and vicarious reinforcement, and added the construct of self-efficacy (which is governed by attention, retenion, production, and motivation). Bandura stated that self-efficacy is domain- and situational-specific and depends on outcome expectancy of physical, social, and self-evaluation results. Individuals are products of their surrounding social system as well as producers thereof. Human agency has intentionality, forethought, self-reactiveness, and self-reflectiveness. A triadic reciprocal causation exists among environment, intrapersonal factors, and behavior. Social cognitive theory is applied in technology adoption and information searching. Attribution theory is a related concept that focuses on a person's self-perception of his or her ability and control to do a task; is their success in information use a matter of self-compentency or just dumb luck?

- Social phenomenology studies how people construct meaning cognitively and perceptually, particularly within the context of a problematic situation. It also explores common understandings. The theory also studies reciprocal interactions between human action and situational structuring. Schutz constructed three types of people based on their assumptions and systems of relevances: man on the street with "recipe knowledge," "well-informed" citizen, and expert.

Fisher, Erdelez, and McKechnie (2005) collated seventy-two theories and models of information behavior and provided short descriptions of each. The following ones are applicable to examining student information behaviors.

- The affective domain tends to initiate, maintain, and terminate cognitive behaviors. Affective load may be formulated as uncertainty (which is fueled by frustration, anxiety, and anger) multiplied by felt time press; when the affective load is too high, it negatively impacts information behavior.
- Some theories focus on searching strategies. Berrypicking refers to the idea that each piece of information found modifies the seeker's direction; this process may include hunting from citation to citation and browsing serendipity. Optimal foraging focuses on a seeker's ability to choose among alterative strategies based on the value and cost of each direction; for instance, how one can get the best results with the least time and effort.
- Another set of theories examines group impact on information behavior. Communities of practice are self-identified groups with a common goal who develop a shared body of knowledge for self- and group improvement. Collective action dilemmas occur when one person does not contribute to the group's information collection but does draw from it (the bane of some group projects). Another dilemma can emerge when the collected information leads to poorer overall quality than information collected by one person.
- Some theories deal with information interchange: between the information provider (such as the school librarian) and the information user. The information provider tends to focus on the issue and wants to help users become better informed; the information user has a specific need, which may be complex. Another model focuses on a user's willingness to return to an information provider; factors that lead to return business include interest in the question, good listening skills, effective use of open questions, and ability to determine the underlying information need.
- Culture also impacts information behavior. Hall noted that culture impacts the level of context in communication (such as group assumptions and tacit knowledge versus the message itself) and differing concepts of time (including speed of communication, sequencing of action, and the differ-

ence between linear and simultaneous information). Hofstede identified five dimensions that differentiate culture and impact ensuing information behavior: power distance (such as between the student and the teacher), individualism versus collectivism (which impacts group work), uncertainty avoidance (which impacts the user's need for just the right answer), gendered roles, and long- or short-term orientation (which can impact persistence).

More details about some of these theories and models may be found at:

- http://www.slideshare.net/guestab667e/information-seeking-theories-and-models,
- http://searchuserinterfaces.com/book/sui_ch3_models_of_information_seeking.html,
- http://informationr.net/ir/9-1/paper163.html, Xie_article

OPTIMIZING INFORMATION-SEEKING STRATEGIES

A Question of Behavior Quality

In describing information behaviors, quality has not been the focus in this chapter. However, each decision does require the person to make a qualitative (and sometimes quantitative) judgment. However, the person himself or herself might not make high-quality decisions. Furthermore, his or her information behavior might not be efficient or effective. Figure 3.2 illustrates dimensions of effective information behavior.

The goal is minimum effort (and time) for optimum (relevant, authoritative, complete) results. The typical paradigm is that the more time and effort that one exerts, the better the results. Novice information users tend to be ineffective, and expert ones tend to have a broad repertoire of effective searching and using strategies. While repeated practice can improve imformation behaviors, especially with effective self-reflection and self-regulation, instruction and other outside interventions are intended to speed up that improvement process. This section explains how different kinds of resources are organized so that users can optimize their information behaviors.

A Note about Information Architecture

Information architecture has been defined as "the art and science of organizing information and interfaces to help information seekers solve their information needs efficiently and effectively" (Eichorn, 2005, p. 178). For instance, the comic arts use sequential frames, text "containers," and image conventions as information architectural "tools" to convey meaning. Some-

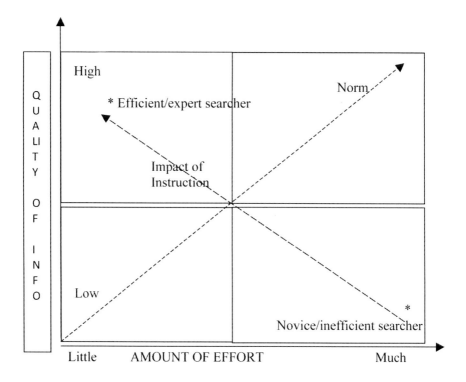

Figure 3.2.   Dimensions of effective information behavior.

times the term "information genre" is used to describe different forms of information. Marshall McLuhan (1954) broadened this concept to assert that "the medium is the message," recognizing how format impacts how one perceives the content. Expert information users know the "grammar" of different source architectures and can locate and interpret information more effectively leveraging this knowledge.

Searching Print Resources

Even print resources vary in their informational structure. Students need to learn how to navigate their different interfaces, as well as generate information using these protocols. So it is important that the library provide examples of these and explain how to use them.

Monographs. Most monographs (i.e., one-volume books) have a table of contents that sequentially lists the major topics and an index that facilitates searching for specific topics and authors. Within each chapter, headings (often indicated by a larger boldface font) identify the main ideas, and subheadings detail aspects of each main idea. Captioned pictures provide a visual representation of nearby concepts, and tables or charts offer an efficient way to organize and summarize facts and figures. Expert information users typically flip through the monograph to ascertain its content and arrangement. In addition, reference monographs often provide a preface or introduction that gives the reader guidelines on how to use the volume; time spent on reading the preface is a good investment because it frontloads the searching strategy.

Multivolume books. Encyclopedias constitute the main example of multivolume books. Sometimes the table of contents or index in each volume is comprehensive, but other times those access tools pertain to just that one volume. Some multivolume resources have a separate index volume.

Series. When several volumes are published, usually at different times, with a linked theme, the set is called a series. Typical series include books about geographic regions or biographies (e.g., presidents). Publishers usually use a consistent layout and appearance for the entire series in order to "brand" it and to facilitate information search and use. Normally, each volume is self-sufficient so the reader does not have to consult other volumes.

Journals and magazines. Most journals and magazines are published at regular intervals, from daily to yearly. Each issue normally has the same format and layout, again to brand it and facilitate its use. Generally, all journals and magazines have a table of contents, which may cluster different types of articles such as featured (main) ones, regular columns, news, letters to the editor, organizational matters, and miscellaneous items. Usually the cover or featured article is the first main one and may have more images than other articles. "Trade" or commercial magazines recover much of their printing cost through advertisements; the favored placements are the back cover and inside the front cover. Sometimes an ad is placed alongside an associated article so that a story about the oil industry might have a car ad next to it. Scholarly journals tend to have longer articles and fewer (or no) advertisements; they might also look "denser" (i.e., have smaller font size and fewer graphics), typically because journal budgets may be small so printing costs have to be minimized. Most scholarly journals have a typical sequence within each article: introduction, need, literature review, research question, methodology, findings, discussion, conclusion, recommendations, and bibliography. Expert users use this pattern to quickly determine the topic and approach in order to determine whether to pursue reading the entire article.

Newspapers. Newspapers depend on layout norms to guide how they place articles. Occasionally, newspapers will have a brief table of contents that highlights features in different sections of the newspaper, especially if those features shift daily (e.g., crossword puzzles). Newspapers with different sections (i.e., separate set of newsprint sheets) cluster similar news for faster information retrieval (such as sports, business, entertainment). Generally, the main story is on the front page at the top right-hand corner. The term "above the fold" refers to oversized newspapers that are folded over top to bottom for easier reading; more important articles are located above the fold. Articles on the right-hand side (the odd-numbered pages) tend to be more important than those on the left-hand side. When editors want to "bury" a news item, they will likely put it in a second or third section toward the back of the section, on the lower half of an even-numbered page near the "gutter" (the line between the two facing pages). The expert information user knows these protocols and can determine the newspaper editors' relative priority of the news.

Searching the World Wide Web

As noted before, many users prefer going online to search for information, largely because of convenience (if they have easy Internet access) and the probability that they will find information. Because the Google search engine accesses more sources than any other search engine and is easy to use, it has become the de facto default online access tool. Sadly, quantity sometimes outweighs quality, so that even if the information is not necessarily accurate or really relevant, the fact that there *is* information might satisfy the casual searcher. On the other hand, too much information can overwhelm users and cause them to stop at the first page just as a coping mechanism. Only as they delve into the resource will they be disappointed and have to search again (*re*-search) (Todd, 2003).

There are dozens of search engines, each of which uses algorithms to search stored information from websites in order to satisfy the inquirer's parameters. Generally, the inquirer types in key terms that try to capture his or her information need. Most search engines combine significant words (ignoring words such as "the" or "an"), which tend to be nouns since most searching is topical. In that respect, natural language, such as a sentence, does not produce the most effective results. Each search engine has a protocol for:

- identifying phrases (usually a set of parentheses or quotation marks);
- combining terms (such as Boolean operators or plus signs);
- using truncation and "wild cards" to get more results (such as asterisks or question marks to get different forms or spelling variations);
- delimiting factors (such as reading level, file type, language, size, and currency).

Most search engines list the results in order of relative relevance and popularity, but alternative orders may be possible, such as currency or number of times the source is cited. The order can also be impacted by payments by the website owner (similar to placing an advertisement) or concerted efforts to go to the website repeatedly in order to increase its popularity ranking. Little-known educational research might have just the right information but is outranked by more commercial sources. Even the sequence of the search terms impacts the results, which is a good exercise for users to do in order to compare the hits. Expert searchers know which protocols for each search engine used, and they know how to match the search engine with the information task. For instance, http://www.thesearchenginelist.com/ notes the focus of different search engines (e.g., http://go.com is a family-friendly search engine owned by Disney, blogsphere keeps track of blog content, and wazap focuses on gaming).

If a student has a vague idea about a research topic, such as current India, then a web directory is an effective search strategy. Yahoo (http://dir.yahoo.com) and the Open Directory Project (http://dmoz.org) are the most well-known ones. The Internet Public Library (http://www.ipl.org) is a librarian-vetted directory, which provides subset directories for children and for teens. Another librarian-generated directory, KidsClick (http://www.kidsclick.org), is considered a "classic" web directory for children. Web directories usually show major headings and popular subheadings on the home page, so that users can easily click on the topic that sounds most relevant. The linked page usually lists associated linked websites and may note even more detailed subheadings (that is, narrower topics). Cluster search engines combine the convenience of single-entry access with directory-like headings that narrow the topic; representative examples include Yippy (http://www.yippy.com) and FirstGov (http://www.usa.gov); the former is especially useful for students who have to do a research project within a broad theme (such as the Middle Ages). Bamboo Dirt (http://dirt.projectbamboo.org/) offers a number of web-based research tools, from which the user can choose, depending on the information needed; this compendium works particularly well when the user has identified the information need and the type of data that can satisfy that need.

Searching Database Aggregators

Most states in the United States underwrite subscriptions to database aggregator services such as Ebsco and ProQuest for public and school libraries. Librarians encourage their use because the resources are professionally selected and indexed. In addition, some database aggregators such as Ebsco's Student Research Center and ProQuest's Big Chalk target K–12 audiences, providing developmentally appropriate sources that support typical K–12 curriculum. For some students, the initial task of choosing one of several databases can be challenging. In some cases, the vendor provides an information dialog box to explain the content and scope of that database.

These databases can be searched in much the same way as a search engine, but they usually provide an option for easy keyword combining that incorporates specific field designations such as author or journal title. Current databases also tend to provide several delimiters such as date and type of document. Once the result list appears, the user can further refine the search and even save the desired sources. Some databases include "search similar articles," which usually entails using the same defining terms, but results may be unpredictable. Instead, expert users try to find one resource that appears to be relevant and then use the associated keywords to refine their search and retrieve additional appropriate articles.

Students can also examine the bibiographies of relevant articles to trace back other people's contributions; this practice works best for pre-reviewed scholarly efforts. In that respect, Google Scholar (http://scholar.google.com) works well because it lists relevant articles, usually starting with the most cited article. It should be noted, though, that these citation practices are used for colleagiate research rather than K–12, though school librarians might well point out these strategies to their teacher colleagues.

Considering Other Literacies

As mentioned already, information is presented in many formats. In recognition of that fact, Google's search engine, for one, provides shortcuts for users to search for images (including maps) and YouTube videos. Google's advanced image search options enable the user to determine file size, type of image, principal color, and currency. The expert information user matches the kind of information with the most effective format. For instance, a process such as the reason for seasons might be best understood by viewing a video. Visual representations of Hindu gods convey rich information that might be missed in a textual description. Poetry gains depth when read orally, and of course most musical compositions are meant to be played in order to be fully appreciated.

Visual literacy predates textual literacy and has reemerged as an important literacy, especially in a global digital society. Visual literacy, as with other literacies, includes one's ability to comprehend, interpret, and produce visual information. These days, the use of technology tools is part of visual literacy. Content is created through the purposeful use of artistic elements: dots, line, space, color, texture, scale, dimension, and movement. These elements are combined according to visual principles of balance, symmetry, contrast, proportion, pattern, rhythm, emphasis, unity, and variety. It should be noted that, while principles of visual "language" are universal, their meaning may be culturally defined. For instance, the color yellow has different connotations in different cultures, and the visual interpretation of an owl also carries different meanings according to each culture. As information users understand these principles, they can better discern a visual message and how it tries to influence the viewer.

Media literacy concerns itself with mass media messages and their under-lying agendas. In 2002 the Center for Media Literacy developed core con-cepts about media literacy:

- All media messages are constructed.
- Media messages are constructed using a creative language that has unique rules.
- Media messages are constructed to gain profit or power.
- Media have embedded values and points of view.
- Different people perceive the same message differently.

Information users need to analyze how the message is made, the message's content and framework, and the message's production value for them to determine how to respond, if at all, to the message.

Aural literacy deals with sense-making of sounds. It should be noted that oral literacy refers to speech, and musical literacy addresses both sound and notation. Aural litearcy involves hearing (being aware of sound), identifying a sound, and comprehending its meaning through processing and intepreting it. By its nature, sound is ephemeral, existing within the context of time and space, but recorded sound can be experienced separate from its original setting.

Manipulating Information

More attention is placed on locating and comprehending information than on its extraction and transformation. The former activities emphasize the consu-mer role of information use and underplay the person's proactive role. How-ever, the ability to extract the relevant details to satisfy the information need to complete the information task requires critical thinking and decision mak-ing. Furthermore, if several information sources are incorporated, they need to be compared and synthesized. The information user has to determine the type of notes to take (e.g., Cornell, outline form, spreadsheet, extracted quotes), the format of notes (e.g., index cards, word processing document, photo, highlighted photocopy), and the degree of detail to capture (Shenton, 2010). The underlying question that the user has to answer is: what is the most effective way to represent the needed information? These decisions depend on the ultimate task or product, such as a presentation or a report, and the audience for that product, such as the teacher, a class, or a community agency.

The information user not only has to consider the content but also needs to know how to communicate that content, which may entail learning how to create a podcast or design a web page. While teachers spend years instructing students in writing composition skills, much less time is spent in technological skills. However, as noted in the discussion of comprehending information expressed in different formats, information users have to be able to reproduce those formats as well as "consume" them. Just as writing is the "flip side" of reading, so is filmmaking the flip side of viewing a film, and so forth for other media. Beginning information users tend to focus on the media itself; for instance, beginning PowerPoint users tend to explore word art, transition options, and ways to insert media. Only after they feel comfortable with the media itself do they focus attention on the content, determining the most effective way to present that content within the framework of the media.

CONSTRUCTING QUESTIONS

Asking questions is a vital part of information seeking: it begs an answer, it allows for modification in response to findings, it aids in comprehension, it fosters self-regulation, and it invites conversation. Thus, throughout the process of interacting with information, questions arise because some piece of information is lacking or because the stimulus conflicts with existing information (e.g., a man biting a dog); the mind is trying to reestablish equilibrium. The central issue is clear communication between the information seeker and the potential source of information. A question asks for information, either for clarification (What does Q.E.D. mean?), for understanding (How does the electoral college choose the president?), for evaluation (What is this author's reputation?), or for confirmation (Is it true that Olympia is the capital of Washington?).

The question that thus arises needs to match the informational need: "Why is the man biting the dog?" may match better than "Does the man have canine teeth?" Existing mental schema, vocabulary, and prior experience help craft the form of the question. This meshing of minds requires a common understanding in order to transmit the needed information. Taking a metacognitive look at information seeking using the Big6 research process (Eisenberg & Berkowitz, 1990) as a model, generic process questions might include:

Task Definition

1. Frame the query or assignment. What am I supposed to do? What problem am I trying to solve?
2. Identify the information needed. What do I need to know? What kind of information should I gather?

Information-Seeking Strategies

1. Identify possible sources. Where am I likely to find the answer?
2. Select the sources. Which source is best for answering the question or solving the problem?

Location and Access

1. Locate the source. Where can I find it?
2. Locate the information within the source. What information is within the source? How do I find it?

Use of Information

1. Comprehend the information: read, listen, view. How do I "get at" the information?
2. Extract the useful information. What part of the source is useful? How do I document my findings?

Synthesis

1. Organize the information. What is the logical way to put the findings together?
2. Present the information. What is the most effective way to share the findings?

Evaluation

1. Complete the task. Did I answer the question? Did I solve the problem? Did I do the assignment fully?
2. Assess the process and the product. How could I improve?

While it is useful to share these questions with information seekers, it is important to convey that these steps may be revisited and repositioned depending on the context, task, strategy, and needs of each individual. Moreover, evaluative questions arise at every point, not just at the end.

The skill of posing questions *throughout the information-seeking process* is often undervalued and undertaught. To ask quality, higher-level questions requires explicit instruction. With their knowledge of information sources and processes, school librarians can be instrumental in helping youth ask questions that will give them the answers they want and need.

ASSESSING INFORMATION BEHAVIORS

Throughout this chapter, characteristics of effective information users have been described. Table 3.1 provides a simple rubric for assessing information behavior. The rubric can be used to spark discussion about the elements of information behaviors and brainstorm strategies that meet different information needs. Students can use it to self-assess their efforts and point out strategies for improving their information actions. Most importantly, though, by assessing the school community's information behaviors, school librarians can identify common areas of need so they can design effective interventions that can support information users at their point of need—and can design instruction that frontloads information behaviors to optimize the experience and the results.

REFERENCES

Abrahamson, J., Fisher, K., Turner, A., Durrance, J., & Turner, T. (2008). Lay information mediary behavior uncovered: Exploring how nonprofessionals seek health information for themselves and others online. *Journal of the Medical Library Association, 96*(4), 310–323.

Agosto, D. (2011). Young adults' information behavior: What we know so far and where we need to go from here. *Journal of Research on Libraries and Young Adults, 2*(1). Retrieved from http://www.yalsa.ala.org/jrlya/2011/11/young-adults%E2%80%99-information-behavior-what-we-know-so-far-and-where-we-need-to-go-from-here/.

Agosto, D., & Hughes-Hassell, S. (2006). Toward a model of the everyday life information needs of urban teenagers, part 1: Theoretical model. *Journal of the American Society for Information Science and Technology, 57*(10), 1394–1406.

American Association for the Advancement of Science. (1999). *Dialogue on early childhood science, mathematics, and technology education.* Washington, DC: American Association for the Advancement of Science.

Ames, P. (2003). The role of learning style in university students' computer attitudes: Implications relative to the effectiveness of computer-focused and computer-facilitated instruction. (Doctoral dissertation, The Claremont Graduate University). ProQuest Dissertations and Theses (AAT 3093249).

Bailey, E. (2008). Constance Mellon demonstrated that college freshmen are afraid of academic libraries. *Evidence Based Library & Information Practice, 3*(3), 94–97.

Bilal, D. (2012). Ranking, relevance judgment, and precision of information retrieval on children's queries: Evaluation of Google, Yahoo!, Bing, Yahoo! Kids, and Ask Kids. *Journal of the American Society for Information Science & Technology, 63*(9), 1879–1896.

Borgman, C., Hirsh, S., & Walter, V. (1995). Children's searching behavior on browsing and keyword online catalogs: The Science Library Catalog Project. *Journal of the American Society for Information Science, 46*(9), 663–684.

Branch, J. (2001). Information-seeking processes of junior high school students. *School Libraries Worldwide, 7*(1), 11–27.

Center for Media Literacy. (2002). *Literacy for the 21st century.* Malibu, CA: Center for Media Literacy.

Chapman, E. & Pendleton, V. (1995). Knowledge gap, information-seeking and the poor. *The Reference Librarian, 49/50*, 135-145.

Dobbs, D. (2011). Beautiful brains. *National Geographic, 220*(4), 37–59.

Dresang, E. (1999). *Radical change: Books for youth in a digital age.* New York: H. W. Wilson.

Table 3.1.   Information Behavior Analysis Rubric

	4	3	2	1
Data Gathering	Method is appropriate and justified. Method incorporates technology significantly and appropriately.	Method is appropriate. Method incorporates technology, but not centrally.	Method is appropriate. Little or no technology is incorporated.	Method is not appropriate. No technology used.
Data Findings	Description appears accurate, specific, nuanced, and thorough. Language is free from bias and judgment of behavior.	Description seems generally accurate and specific. Language is generally free from bias and judgment of behavior.	Description is vague and uneven in quality. Language is biased.	Scant description.
Interpretation	Interpretation is data-driven, specific, logical, thorough, and insightful. Interpretation makes excellent use of an information-seeking model/ theory and information literacy model.	Interpretation is data-driven and logical and covers most points. It contains specific ideas. Interpretation is linked to an information-seeking model/ theory and an information literacy model.	Interpretation is uneven and vague. Several issues are not addressed. Interpretation mentions an information-seeking model/ theory *or* an information literacy model.	Little inter-pretation. No/ little mention of an information-seeking model /theory, and no/little men-tion of an information literacy model.
Implications	Implications are sound, insightful, and well-justified. Implications focus on education or library programs.	Implications are feasible and justified. Implications focus on education or library programs.	Implications are not sound or well-justified. Implications are vague.	One or two implications with no justification.

Mechanics and Completeness	Clear organization, well-written, no mechanical errors. All aspects are present, and all were submitted on time. All work follows the directions closely. Citations are accurate and complete.	Generally well-written, satisfactory organization, few mechanical errors. Most aspects are present. Most work followed directions. Citations are accurate and complete.	Adequate writing but unclear, some mechanical errors. Some aspects are not submitted or are incomplete. Directions were not well followed. Citations are complete.	Poor writing, submitted late. Directions are not followed. Citations are incomplete.

Dresang, E., & Koh, K. (2009). Change theory, youth information behavior, and school libraries. *Library Trends, 58*(1), 26–50.

Eichorn, F. (2005). *Who owns the data?* Mustang, OK: Tate.

Eisenberg, M., & Berkowitz, R. (1990). *Information program solving: The Big Six approach to library and information skills instruction.* Norwood, NJ: Ablex.

Farmer, L. (2003). *Student success and library media programs.* Wetsport, CT: Libraries Unlimited.

Fisher, K., Erdelez, S., & McKechnie, L. (Eds.). (2005). *Theories of information behavior.* Medford, NJ: Information Today.

Flanagan, A., & Metzger, M. (2010). *Kids and credibility: An empirical examination of youth, digital media use, and information credibility.* Cambridge, MA: MIT Press.

Foss, E., Druin, A., Brewer, R., Lo, P., Sanchez, L., Golub, E., & Hutchinson, H. (2012). Children's search roles at home: Implications for designers, researchers, educators, and parents. *Journal of the American Society for Information Science & Technology, 63*(3), 558–573.

Gasser, U., Cortesi, S., Malik, M., & Lee, A. (2012). *Youth and digital media: From credibility to information quality.* Cambridge, MA: Berkman Center for Internet & Society. Retrieved from http://ssrn.com/abstract=2005272.

Gross, M. (1999). Imposed queries in the school library media center. *Library & Information Science Research, 21*(4), 501–521.

Harris, R., & Dewdney, P. (1994). *Barriers to information.* Westport, CT: Greenwood.

Head, A. (2013). Project information literacy: What can be learned about the information-seeking behavior of today's college students? *Association of College and Research Libraries Proceedings.* Chicago: Association of College and Research Libraries.

Heinström, J. (2006). Fast surfing for availability or deep diving into quality—motivation and information seeking among middle and high school students. *Information Research, 11*(4), paper 265. http://InfroamtionR.net/ir/114/paper265.html.

Henry, K. (2005). *Literacy skills and strategies while searching for information on the Interent: A comprehensive review and synthesis of research.* Storrs: University of Connecticut.

Kuhlthau, C. (2004). *Seeking meaning: A process approach to library and information services* (2nd ed.). Westport, CT: Libraries Unlimited.

Large, A., Nesset, V., & Beheshti, J. (2008). Children as information seekers: What researchers tell us. *New Review of Children's Literature & Librarianship, 14*(2), 121–140.

Lazonder, A., & Rouet, J. (2008). Information problem solving instruction: Some cognitive and metacognitive issues. *Computers in Human Behavior, 24,* 753–765.

Lien, C. (2000). Approaches to Internet searching: An analysis of student in grades 2 to 12. *Journal of Instruction Delivery Systems, 14*(3), 6–13.

Loh, C., & Williams, M. (2003). What's in a web site? Students' perceptions. *Journal of Research on Technology in Education, 34*(3), 351–363.

Lu, Y. (2010). Children's information seeking in coping with daily-life problems: An investigation of fifth- and sixth-grade students. *Library & Information Science Research, 32*, 77–88.

Lubans, J. (1999). When students hit the surf: What kids really do on the Internet. And what they want from librarians. *School Library Journal, 45*(9), 144–147.

McLuhan, M. (1954). *Understanding media: The extensions of man.* Cambridge, MA: MIT Press.

Meyers, E., Fisher, K., & Marcoux, E. (2009). Making sense of an information world: The everyday-life information behavior of preteens. *Library Quarterly, 79*(3), 301–341.

Nesset, V. (2013). Two representations of the research process: The preparing, searching, and using (PSU) and the beginning, acting and telling (BAT) models. *Library & Information Science Research, 35*(2), 97–106.

Oakleaf, M., & Owen, P. (2010). Closing the 12-13 gap: School and college librarians supporting 21st century learners. *Teacher Librarian, 37*(4), 52–58.

Purcell, K., Rainie, L., Heaps A., Buchanan, J., Friedrich, L., Jacklin, A., Chen, C., Zickuhr, K. (2012). *How teens do research in the digital world.* Pew Internet & American Life Project. Retrieved from http://pewinternet.org/~/media//Files/Reports/2012PIP_TeacherSurveyReportWithMethodology110112.pdf.

Savolainen, Reijo, & Kari, Jarkko. (2004). Placing the Internet in information source horizons. *Library and Information Science Research, 26*, 415–433.

Schroeder, R. (2009). Both sides now: Librarians looking at information literacy from high school and college. Tips. *Educators' Spotlight Digest, 4*(1). Retrieved from http://files.eric.ed.gov/fulltext/EJ899891.pdf.

Shenton, A. (2010). Information capture: A key element in information behaviour. *Library Review, 59*(8), 585–595.

Shenton, A., & Dixon, P. (2004). Issues arising form youngsters' information-seeking behavior. *Library & Information Science Research, 26*, 177–200.

Todd, R. (2003). Adolescents of the information age: Patterns of information seeking and use, and implications for information professionals. *School Libraries Worldwide, 9*(2), 27–46.

Vansickle, S. (2002). Tenth graders' search knowledge and use of the web. *Knowledge Quest, 30*(4), 33–37.

Wilson, T. (Ed.). (2013). *Theory in information behaviour research.* Sheffield, UK: Eiconics.

Winters, K. (2008). *Adolescent brain development and drug abuse.* Philadelphia, PA: Treatment Research Institute.

Chapter Four

Developing Resource Collections

Informational needs reflect a wide range of information in various formats. Research information is the focus of the content to be covered in this chapter, but the range of formats will be addressed. The sources should address the information needs of school members with special needs such as English language learners and people with disabilities. Specific criteria, including for digital materials, apply to reference sources. Representative tools and policies are noted. As a sidebar, the concept of humans as sources of reference information—and how school librarians can identify such resources—is discussed.

WHAT IS A REFERENCE RESOURCE?

The American Library Association defines a reference book as: (1) a book designed by the arrangement and treatment of its subject matter to be consulted for definite items of information rather than to be read consecutively; (2) a book whose use is restricted to the library building (Levine-Clark & Carter, 2013). This definition may be broadened to include reference sources in various formats. These materials offer invaluable information for researchers and librarians. Regardless of the source, the user needs to examine it carefully in terms of its content and retrieval method. In the final analysis, a good reference source is one that answers questions, and a poor reference source is one that fails to answer questions.

PROFILE OF THE TYPICAL REFERENCE RESOURCE

Usually the first kinds of resources that people think of as reference include encyclopedias, dictionaries, and almanacs. Each of them, along with several other types of reference, has the following characteristics:

- locates facts;
- is arranged for quick retrieval of information (e.g., alphabetical, chrono-logical, tables);
- is used for consultation rather than for continuous reading;
- is used frequently;
- may be unique in coverage;
- may be costly;
- is usually restricted to library use.

Additional optional criteria for reference materials might include timeliness, usage (e.g., an index), and substantive unique features (e.g., charts, dia-grams). For instance, a current yearbook of consumer product reviews might be considered a reference book while older editions might not be as useful. On the other hand, a dictionary of literary terms might be old but still a valuable reference tool. In *Library Journal*'s 1999 list of top ten reference sources of the century, most of the titles remain very influential, and they could all be useful in high school libraries:

- *Webster's Third New International Dictionary*
- *World Almanac*
- *Times Atlas of the World*
- *Statistical Abstract of the U.S.*
- *Oxford English Dictionary*
- *Encyclopedia Britannica/Americana* (tied)
- *Reader's Guide to Periodical Literature/InfoTrac* (both indexes to period-icals)
- *Facts on File*
- *Encyclopedia of Associations*
- *Physicians' Desk Reference*

Occasionally, a general overview book, such as a fancy art history volume, might be found on the reference shelves, largely because of its cost or size. Librarians could just as easily have an oversize and/or restricted use set of shelves in order to differentiate the materials' intended use. Indeed, most school libraries are migrating to a small, "lean" ready-reference section, integrating multivolume series, such as animal encyclopedias, into the gener-al shelves. In some cases, the books may be marked as "in-library" use only, which may result in some confusion at the circulation desk for students who equate general collection with circulating collection. On the other hand, too often large reference sections are underused, so librarians would prefer users finding the materials and being disappointed that the items must stay in house than not finding the resources at all. Furthermore, some librarians have liberal circulation policies relative to reference and reference-wannabe items, particularly if users have limited access to the library. For those cases when many students would want to consult the same volume, the librarian simply places that item on a reserve shelf. All of these issues point out the need for clarification of reference materials and policies about their arrangement and use. The following are representative ready-reference website directories:

- Internet Public Library: http://www.ipl.org/IPLBrowse/GetSubject?vid= 13&tid=6996&parent=0
- New York State Library: http://www.nysl.nysed.gov/reference/readyref. htm
- Internet Library for Librarians: http://www.itcompany.com/inforetriever/
- Refseek: http://www.refseek.com/directory/

TYPES OF REFERENCE SOURCES

Reference sources tend to be categorized by their type of usage, as detailed below. As such, they have unique characteristics. Reference sources are also considered in terms of scope: either general (such as a generic dictionary) or subject-specific (such as a gazetteer).

Each library contains a core set of reference sources that are consulted daily, particularly to answer quick facts. These materials are known colloquially as "ready reference." Librarians need to familiarize themselves with these basic tools so they can use them efficiently. Increasingly, reference collections consist solely of ready reference rather than deep references such as specialized encyclopedias. Of course, what is ready reference in a medical library might be considered deep reference in a school setting. Furthermore, online reference collections may include more specialized resources, including aggregator databases; a reference web page may serve as a directory, with one link to ready reference, another to databases, and a third set listed by curricular areas.

This section details major types of ready reference: noting their content, critical features, means of access, sample titles, and representative questions to be answered by each.

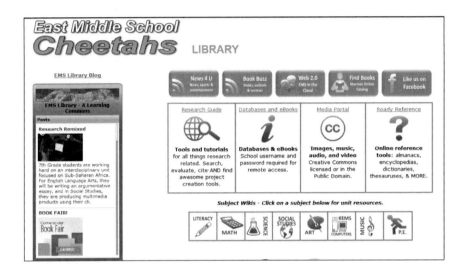

Figure 4.1. Sample library portal.

Encyclopedias

Encyclopedias constitute the most obvious reference source. They provide background information, sometimes with subtopics and cross-references. Most encyclopedias are arranged alphabetically, with quick access through indexes found either at the end of each volume or as a separate volume. Most encyclopedias are multivolume, but a few, such as the *Columbia Encyclopedia*, may consist of a single volume. Furthermore, some publishers may intermix the terms "encyclopedia" and "dictionary" for alphabetically arranged references that have entries that may be one to several paragraphs in length. Encyclopedias may be general in scope or subject-specific. The latter are usually limited to high school reference collections where even there such resources may be underused if not actively promoted by school librarians. Representative titles include:

- *World Book* (for third grade up) (also available in Spanish)
- *Britannica* (for sixth grade up) (also available in Spanish)
- *Grolier* (for third grade up)
- *Catholic Encyclopedia* (for ninth grade up)
- *Encyclopedia of World Biography* (for sixth grade up)
- *McGraw-Hill Encyclopedia of Science of Technology* (for ninth grade up)
- *Grove Music Online* (for ninth grade up) (this title used to be called a dictionary even though it is several volumes)

Typical questions answered by encyclopedias include:

- What is socialism's impact?
- What were the causes of the Cold War?
- How do hurricanes form?
- What is the life cycle of a frog?
- What were the main features of each major art movement in history?

When evaluating and using encyclopedias, look for some of these added criteria:

- How is article content sequenced? Some give a summary and then go into more depth. Some have a gradated reading level, starting with simpler language and progressing to more complex text.
- Are articles signed?
- Do articles include a bibliography?
- How often is content updated?
- Do digital encyclopedias have hotlinks, including news or other content updates?
- Do digital encyclopedias include sound and video?
- Is the encyclopedia available in non-English? It should be noted that Spanish vocabulary and grammar practices vary among countries. Mexican publishers and editors are probably a better match for U.S. readers.

Dictionaries

A dictionary is an alphabetical list of words. Generally, each entry includes definitions, pronunciation, origin (etymology), and usage. Some dictionaries include charts, diagram, maps, or other illustrations. Some dictionaries include added facts, such as lists of higher education institutions, rhymes, or grammar rules. Along with subject-specific dictionaries, other types of specialized dictionaries include synonyn/antonym, slang, and abbreviations. Dictionaries also vary in terms of depth, varying from pocket size to one-volume desk size to multivolume. Unabridged dictionaries are supposedly word inclusive; the most comprehensive dictionary is *Webster's Third Collegiate Dictionary*. Other representative titles include:

- *Oxford English Dictionary* (best source for etymology)
- *Merriam-Webster Dictionaries*
- *Webster's New World Children's Dictionary*
- *Roget's Thesaurus* (note that the original version was arranged thematically, similarly to an ontology; most thesauri are arranged alphabetically)
- *Webster's Dictionary of English Usage*

- *Random House Historical Dictionary of American Slang*
- HarperCollins series of bilingual dictionaries
- *Webster's Official Crossword Puzzle Dictionary*
- *Acryonyms, Initialisms, and Abbreviations Dictionary* (Gale)
- *Facts on File Visual Dictionary*
- *Columbia Gazetteer of the World* (dictionary of geographic terms)
- *Glossary of Literary Terms*
- *MedlinePlus Medical Dictionary*

Typical questions answered by dictionaries include:

- What is the origin of the word "catastrophe"?
- How do you pronounce "sarsaparilla"?
- What is the plural form of "cactus"?
- What does the acronym NASA stand for?
- What English words starting with Q do not have a U immediately following?

When evaluating and using dictionaries, look for some of these added criteria:

- reading level (note that a dictionary for primary grades should differ from one targeted to adult English language learners);
- variant spellings;
- pronunciation keys;
- grammatical information;
- inclusion of sample sentences;
- order of definitions: some dictionaries list definitions in order by popularity, while others order them chronologically, so it's best to read the preface to ascertain the order.

Non-English dictionaries have additional properties that should be considered. England produces several good bilingual dictionaries (e.g., Harrap's); however, they use British spelling, which can confuse U.S. students. Currency is particularly important for bilingual dictionaries because formal and informal vocabulary varies and can make the communicator sound dated or pedantic if the wrong word is chosen. For high school collections, single language dictionaries, such as *Larouse Petit Dictionnaire Francais* and *Es-Pasa diccionario de la lengua española—para estudiantes de español*, can be useful for more advanced students. Foreign language dictionaries should provide simple definitions and examples of use in a sentence. When locating a word in another language, it's a good idea to then verify the word choice by looking at the word in the target language and seeing what English word it references. For instance, the French word for "disk" is "disque" (no surprise), but three words are associated with the word "disque" (in French): "disc," "disk," and "record"; a one-to-one correlation cannot be guaranteed.

Almanacs and Yearbooks

Almanacs and yearbooks are usually annual publications with fast facts and figures in an easy-to-find format. Some give more long-standing data, such as award winners and geographic statistics, and some provide current trends such as economic data. Sometimes chronologies are included in this category. These sources are typically arranged topically, with detailed indexes to facilitate information retrieval. Most have tables and charts that succinctly present statistical data. Middle school libraries should keep a class set of almanacs to teach data analysis skills. Typical titles include:

- *Information Please Almanac*
- *World Almanac*
- *Statesman's Yearbook*
- *Chase's Calendar of Events*
- *Chronology of World History*
- *Leonard Maltin's Video Guide*

Typical questions answered by almanac resources include:

- What's the longest river in the world?
- What were the most important events of the last year?
- What movies did Mel Brooks direct?
- Who has won the Nobel Peace Prize?
- What percentage of the U.S. population have disabilities?

Atlases

An atlas is a methodical collection of maps covering one or more topics. Several types of maps exist: physical, political, thematic, and historic. It should be noted that atlases may focus on animals, astronomy, and even imaginary places. Besides maps, atlases may include glossaries, statistics, illustrations, comparative maps, and text; online atlases may include video and sound clips as well. Information is typically accessed via tables of contents and indexes. Globes are not as popular as they once were, but they can serve as a useful teaching tool in schools; the main limitation is their quick obsolescence. Some indexes refer to places by map coordinates (e.g., G2) and others reference by latitude/longitude. Atlases exemplify the need for currency, except for historical atlases. Indeed, *Shepherd's Historical Atlas*, though dated, remains a valuable source of information. It should be noted that gazetteers (geographical dictionaries) and guidebooks serve as useful complements to atlases for geographic information. It should also be mentioned that online maps have become the preferred format for map information because of their timeliness, flexible scale, and ability to be enriched through customizable features. Nevertheless, school libraries should maintain a core collection of print atlases. Indeed, it is a good idea for middle schools to have a class set of a student version of an atlas (e.g., Hammond's *Discovering Maps*) in order to teach map-reading skills. Key map publishers include the National Geographic Society, Rand McNally, Hammond, and Oxford. Representative titles include:

- *Times Atlas of the World*
- *Oxford Atlas of World History*
- *National Geographic Historical Atlas of the United States*
- *Historical Atlas of Native Americans*
- *Ocean: An Illustrated Atlas*
- *New Atlas of the Moon*
- *Atlas of Endangered Resources*
- Thomas Cook for local maps
- *Imaginary Atlas*
- *Google Earth*

Typical questions answered by atlases include:

- What is Iran's terrain?
- Where was the silk route?
- What is the distance between Paris and Rome?
- What is the relationship between the presence of rivers and the location of cities?
- What is the migration pattern of different birds?

When evaluating and using atlases, look for some of these added criteria:

- Projection: Mercator can be misleading; some people prefer Gall-Peters projection, and several other projection models exist.
- The order of the maps and their scale usually reflects the perspective of the publisher; for instance, U.S. publishers usually start with the Americas and have detailed states maps, unlike British publishers who may favor European countries.
- Spelling preferences (e.g., variants from U.S. spelling): the preface usually explains the usage.
- Keys and legend quality.

- Measurement scale: metric versus English/American.
- Use of color: differentiation should be made by additional methods (e.g., labels, line quality) in order to be accessible for people with color blindness.

Handbooks and Manuals

Handbooks and manuals provide concise facts, often technical, and guides to a specific topic. Manuals, in particular, focus on procedural knowledge and often include diagrams and other illustrations. Access to these sources is usually through the table of contents or index. Representative titles include:

- Chilton's car manuals
- Peterson and Audubon nature guides
- *Masterplots*
- *Handbook of Applied Mathematics*
- *Emily Post's Etiquette*
- *Bartlett's Familiar Quotations*
- *Merck Manual of Diagnosis and Therapy*
- *CRC Handbook of Chemistry and Physics*
- *MLA Handbook for Writers of Research Papers*

Typical questions answered by handbooks and manuals include:

- How do you troubleshoot a printer problem?
- What's the chemical formula for bleach?
- How do you address a queen?
- How do you use a soldering iron?
- What is a difference between a spruce and a pine tree?

Biographical Sources

Reference sources about people can vary from short dictionary entries, which might give just vital statistics and contact information, to long essays. As with encyclopedias and dictionaries, biographical reference sources can be universal or subject-specific, as well as be contemporary or historical. Some directories (i.e., lists) of people may be considered "vanity" publications for which the publisher requires that the listed person pay for the privilege of being included. Similarly, some biographical sources have a bias (usually favorable) while others are more objective and fair-handed. Because most biographical sources are exclusive, it is important to find out the editor's criteria for selection. Most biographical reference sources draw upon other sources of information, which should be cited. In some cases, one person writes all of the entries, while in other cases, numerous contributors write the entries so each one should be evaluated in terms of their authority. Currency can also be important, particulary when contact information is listed, since people move and change jobs. Most biographical sources are targeted to older readers. Representative titles (besides the encyclopedia and dictionary mentioned above) include:

- Marquis' Who's Who series
- *Current Biography* (the cumulative index is a vital part of the source)
- *Dictionary of American Biography* (contains only dead Americans and a few longtime resident foreigners)
- *Cambridge Biographical Encyclopedia* (which is the basis for A&E's on-line Biography website)
- Gale group biography series, especially for literature
- Wilson's biography series
- *Encyclopedia of Associations* (really a directory)
- *Congressional Biographical Directory*
- *Pictorial History of Black Americans*

Typical questions answered by biographical resources include:

- What was the legacy of Karl Marx?
- Who are some Korean mathematicians?
- How can I contact Justin Bieber?
- Who can I network with about stamp collecting?
- What are some literacy criticisms about John Steinbeck?

Guides to Other Sources

Locating high-quality relevant reference sources, and the resources within, can be challenging. School librarians should teach high school students (and their teachers) how to use indexes, abstracts, bibliographies, and concor-dances. All of these tools point to other reference sources, similarly to a library catalog and aggregator databases.

   Indexes. Most reference books have indexes (which might be considered as search engines). Multivolume references normally have a separate volume for the index, which sometimes has to be purchased separately. *Current Biography* and the Gale series exemplify titles that need indexes for users to find the information they need. Magazines also use indexes, such as *National Geographic* and *Scientific American*, and aggregrator databases are built on the idea of indexing.

   Abstracts. Most aggregator databases include abstracts for the docu-ments they index. Such abstracts help users determine the content and quality of the information, and the abstract may suffice for some researchers. University reference sources may include volumes of abstracts and abstract services.

Bibliographies. Lists of vetted sources can give users a good research starting point. Some reference sources include selective bibliographies for each entry or at the end of the volume. Whole volumes can be bibliographes, such as professional collection development selection tools. In any case, bibliographies need to be evaluated in terms of their scope, accuracy, currency, organization, means of selection, and information included for each entry. School librarians routinely create bibliographies, often in the form of pathfinders, which detail research strategies: key terms, background information sources, key reference sources, relevant periodicals, and relevant Dewey Decimal Classification System numbers. LibGuides is a subscription-based application that enables librarians to produce professional-looking bibliographies that can embed multimedia.

Concordances. Concordances alphabetically list the location of significant words that occurred within a work. The best-known concordances list terms for religious works and for Shakespeare's writing. Concordances can be valuable aids for content analysis.

SELECTING REFERENCE SOURCES

Selecting reference resources builds upon general collection development selection policies and practices.

Generic Reference Selection Criteria

As with other materials under consideration, reference sources need to be evaluated in terms of a number of criteria, which should be mentioned in the school library's selection policy.

- Scope or coverage. A statement of purpose can state what subject matter and concepts are addressed, although the ensuing materials sometimes do not fulfill the purpose well. Scope includes geographic and time frames.
- Authority and accuracy. Because reference materials are acquired with the assumption of authority, the credentials of the authors should carry academic, experience, and writing weight. Some publishers focus on reference works, such as Gale Group, Macmillan, and Scribner's, and their reputation almost guarantees that the reference work will be authoritative, accurate, and objective. Especially since reference information can be highly specialized, librarians often have to rely on subject expert reviewers for validation.

- Arrangement and organization. Reference resources need to be arranged for easy retrieval and use, so typical arrangement orders include alphabetical, chronological, or classification (e.g., Dewey Decimal Classification, scientific classification scheme). Tables of content and indexes are usually mandatory, and specialized indexes (e.g., by genre, geographic region) add value. The resource might also have tabs or color-coding to facilitate usage.
- Presentation. What is the overall look of the resource: its layout, typeface, headings, guiding features? What is the length of each entry—and are entries consistent in the type or sequence of information? How are sidebars, charts, and tables used to clarify or add information?
- Special features. Several items can make the research resource unique: images, case studies, tutorials, hyperlinks, sound, video clips, accompanying tools.
- Bibliographies. Most reference resources include bibliographies, either for each entry, chapter, or section or at the end of the work. The bibliographies help verify the accuracy of the resource's information and also guide the reader to further study. If possible, bibliographies themselves should be checked for accuracy, perspective, and currency.
- Curriculum support. The school library's first priority is to support the curriculum, so the librarian should map each reference source onto that curriculum. Resources also support professional practice, so reference materials on counseling and administration, for instance, would be appropriate.
- Developmental issues. Librarians need to determine the reading level and developmental stage of the materials, considering the needs of English language learners and students with special needs.
- Comparison with similar sources. More than one resource is likely to cover the same topic so librarians need to compare the potential resources whenever possible. All of the above criteria need to be considered: scope, arrangement, features, ease of use, accessibility (including issues of special needs). It may be more useful to provide several similar reference materials than copies of the same title in order to offer different approaches.
- Physical condition. Reference books can get heavy handling, so librarians should look for library binding and sturdy paper. If the resource is in good physical condition, sometimes librarians can acquire used titles.
- Demand and usefulness versus cost. Ideally, reference sources provide valuable information across the curriculum, addressing the entire school community. On the other hand, one expensive title might fill a unique information niche for one specific class and thus be worth the price. Making the situation more complex, a teacher might want the librarian to buy a personal favorite reference source; while it is important to be responsive to

faculty needs, the overall collection and funding need to be taken into account.

Selecting Electronic Reference Sources

Increasingly, reference sources are available in both print and digital formats; in fact, some publishers have abandoned print versions altogether (including *Encyclopedia Britannica*). Few products are now in CD-ROM format; they have migrated to web-based documents. Theoretically, digital sources can be updated quickly and can include multimedia features. However, it is important to check those assumptions carefully. Some digital sources are merely scanned versions of print editions, with no added value such as internal search engine, multimedia features, hyperlinks, or even assurance of readability for users with visual impairments. Nor does online format insure lower cost. Many online reference sources are available only on a subscription basis, which gives users access for a specified time frame; usually the library cannot download the entire product to store on a local server. Therefore, if the library lacks funding some year, it no longer has any access to that resource, and so is left with nothing. For that reason, among others (e.g., the quality of hands-on use, need for electricity and equipment), school librarians should maintain print copies of core ready-reference sources: one or two encyclopedias, dictionaries, a thesaurus, atlases, and almanacs.

Digital reference sources should stand up to the standards for evaluating reference sources of any format. In fact, they are held to a higher standard because their digital aspects must also be discerned. However, instead of examining paper and binding quality, librarians need to examine the electronic properties as well as the equipment required to access them. These factors follow:

• Content. Today's users expect full text resources, not just indexing or abstracts. Furthermore, the content needs to be ADA (Americans with Disabilities Act)-compliant (e.g., readable via software for people with vision impairments). Increasingly, content may be available in more than one language, which could be useful depending on the school community's needs.
• Storage. Increasingly, content is stored remotely, in the "cloud," which saves local server space and, hopefully, eliminates worries about theft or maintenance. Resultingly, librarians must ensure that the vendor's storage is stable and dependable. Typically, then, the library is paying for access, not ownership, so that in poor budget years, that access might be eliminated even if subscriptions had been paid for years before. Few vendors permit local archiving options, but librarians can still ask about that possibility; disadvantages of local storage include storage space, corruptibil-

ity, possible crashes, and security and authentication procedures if accessed remotely. In the past, a few references were available as CD-
ROMs, which the library might install onto a local server, but this format
is now considered outdated.

- Interface. Digital resources should be so simple and intuitive to use that no
  guidance is needed. Producers should aim for a consistent look and layout
  to facilitate access and use; for instance, icons should have instant meaning and avoid culture-specific connotations. Librarians should test web-
  based products on several browsers and devices; amazingly, the layout
  may differ, particularly between Mac and PC operating systems. Most
  products should incorporate searching and browsing features so users can
  locate the needed information in several ways. That being said, products
  should include online help such as a starting tutorial and feature-specific
  tips. Certainly, resources should include documentation for technical administrative purposes. As noted above, content and interface must be
  ADA-compliant. If possible, content should be represented in more than
  one format, such as sound and text; similarly, users should be able to
  access content in more than one way (e.g., via keyboard or touch screen).
  These days, librarians should also look for customization options such as
  "branding," differentiated reading levels, or even user-specific tracking
  features. Furthermore, social media features such as the ability to make
  comments or links should be considered. Increasingly, reference resources
  are available in mobile mode (sometimes at extra cost). However, not all
  mobile-ready products have equal interface quality, especially as the user
  needs to drill down though page "layers."
- Output. Can users download, save, and print content? In some cases, information must be viewed and printed page by page rather than as a whole
  file. On the other hand, a few products do not allow the user to print or
  save just a selected portion of a file. Even the file format needs to be
  ascertained: is at saved as a .pdf, .jpg, or .rtf? Is a special plug-in or
  application program needed to read the file?
- Hardware. At this point in time, most digital resources are stored and
  accessed remotely, but librarians might check on possible local server
  options. Nevertheless, digital products usually do require certain technical
  specifications such as processing speed, RAM, bandwidth, and sound and
  video cards. Often, online plug-ins such as Java script and media players
  may be required—and may need to be updated as the vendor also up-
  grades the resource. Can thin clients access the resource? Even though
  Flash is slowly being replaced by HTML5 and other scripting, it should be
  noted that iPads (at the time of this writing) are not Flash-compatible. In
  most cases, products are usually PC/Mac neutral, but mobile operating
  systems now need to be considered. Savvy librarians should have one
  sample of several mobile devices: an iPad, at least one e-reader, an An-

droid or other popular phone-scale device. In that way, library workers can test products for flexible accessibility.

- Software. Technically, the operating system is software. As mentioned above, where librarians had to consider PC and Mac systems, they now have to think about mobile operating systems as well. Also noted above, librarians have to make sure that required plug-ins and other applications can be installed in whatever equipment is used to access the reference resource. With the need for ADA compliance, software is also increasingly interoperative so that assistive technology software (e.g., read-aloud software) can interface with the resource's programming. Librarians should also ask about network software, especially in terms of authentication and other protocols for remote access.
- Cost. Digital resource pricing can be complex. Subscription rates can depend on: the total number of potential users or the number of simultaneous users; in-library or remote access; server options; customization options; single or multisite use; single or multiyear licenses; premium features; service and support options; and so on. Sometimes librarians can get discounts by choosing multiyear agreements or subscribing through a consortium. No standard exists, so each license agreement needs to be negotiated. Aggregator databases can be especially challenging because of packaging options; especially if the company has several product lines, those collections of resources may overlap considerably, so librarians must examine the resource lists carefully. Beyond the vendor costs, librarians also need to factor in technical support costs, along with equipment costs.
- Vendor. School librarians tend to use well-known, stable resource vendors with good reputations, such as EBSCO, ProQuest, and Gale Group. Nevertheless, reference products do change over time, and publishers do get bought out, so librarians should continue to keep an eye on the reference publishing market.

While periodicals themselves are often not considered reference materials per se, largely because their use varies greatly, a strong case can be made that aggregator databases such as EBSCO's Academic Search or SIRS should be considered reference tools because they serve an indexing function, facilitating retrieval of resources used in research. Unlike such index tools of the past, such as the *Reader's Guide to Periodical Literature*, many of today's digital indexes are embedded in the aggrorator database itself, which includes the full text of the targeted resource. Moreover, library catalogs, which may be considered as an index, increasingly provide interfaces that incorporate these indexes so that the user can search both entire products (e.g., a book or DVD) as well as articles within a resource from a single search "bar." Database aggregators demand special attention because of their cost and complexity. Here are guiding questions to ask. However, the most important question is: What information is needed by the target population?

Interface

- How easily can the user find needed info?
- What browsers does it support?
- What navigation tools are available?
- Is searching intuitive and accessible?
- To what depth can the user search for info?
- What HELP function is available?
- Does the source employ an open URL standard?
- How does technical format impact action?
- Can content be downloaded/printed/saved/sent?

Readability

- How clear is the layout?
- Are text and images easy to view?
- Are plug-ins necessary?
- Is content accessible for individuals with special needs?
- Can viewing options be changed?

Technical Requirements

- What kind of system requirements (e.g., operating system, platform, speed, RAM, video, sound) and connectivity are needed?
- Can the resource be networked?
- Is the product web-based?
- Does multiple simultaneous user access impact performance?

Licenses

- What is the scope?
- How complete is content?
- What is the license duration?
- What warranties exist?
- What indemnifications exist?
- What kind of access is available?
- What confidentiality is guaranteed?
- What sharing and archiving are available?
- Is the product disability compliant?

- What statistics are available?
- Is there "leasing with an option to buy"?

Other nondigital multimedia reference sources have format-specific criteria. For instance, video resources must have high fidelity and clear imagery, and the videotape quality itself must withstand heavy use. That said, videotape resources have seldom served as reference sources, except for specialized uses such as local archives. Likewise, realia such as skelton models tend to serve as subject-specific references and are seldom held by the library, though cataloging these items would facilitate their retrieval as needed.

Factors in Choosing Formats

In sum, reference resources may be found in several formats, not only books but also pamphlets, periodicals, online, video, and audio. As with other resources, librarians need to match content, delivery mode, and the needs of the school community. As noted above, multiple formats are usually a good idea for important reference sources. Here are some other specific criteria to address when choosing formats.

- Access vs. ownership. Increasingly, libraries pay for access to digital resources rather than ownership rights. If ownership is important, then print sources should have priority.
- Degree of access. Online access usually extends access in terms of distance, simultaneous use, and time frame convenience. If a resource is available only on one machine, a print version might be more convenient.
- Ease of use. Depending on their experience, print might be easier to navigate for literate users, while digital resources might be easier for online aficionados. It should be noted that even regular computer users might be inefficient keyword searchers.
- Features. Digital resources often include sound and motion and provide more linkages than print resources. On the other hand, print resources might include tables and charts that are easier to read and copy than online ones. Increasingly, aggregator databases provide value-added features such as visual searching, citation formatting, personal saving options, federated full-text locating and linking, and advanced delimiters. Some of these features may cost additional money, so it is important to determine if the potential users really have need for these added functions.
- Need for supporting equipment and staff. As noted above, digital and multimedia resources require equipment and usually electricity. On the other hand, books are often not ADA-compliant without assistive technology. Users may also need staff help to navigate the source, with different

kinds of help depending on the format; for instance, users need to learn how to use a print index and how to use an online navigation bar.

- Need for timeliness. Theoretically, digital resources can be updated continuously, but reality may be a different case. Librarians need to examine sources carefully to determine frequency of changes. Sometimes a print resource is complemented with online updates, which is not very convenient for the user.
- Stability and archiving requirements. No matter the format, over time the material will become worn or deteriorate. Digital resources can be hard to archive—or illegal, depending upon the licensing agreement.
- Special needs. Throughout this chapter, the requirements of individuals with special needs have been mentioned. If possible, reference sources should be available in several formats to accommodate the physical and psychological learning needs and preferences of users.
- Cost. Pricing remains a bottom line consideration. Again, librarians need to weigh one-time costs with annual subscriptions.

HUMANS AS REFERENCE SOURCES

What is the most popular source of information, regardless of information seeker? A trusted human. Children tend to ask parents first, then teachers. As the school community gets to know the librarian and realizes the librarian's expertise, that person becomes a reference source too. Typically, though, the librarian tries to find an authoritative recorded source of information rather than depending on personal memory, if for no other reason than to verify the facts. This process models good research strategies. Nevertheless, librarians can provide a valuable reference service by identifying experts in relevant fields and developing human referral lists, especially for local expertise. Such lists might include political officials, social service providers, career and college counselors, tutors, and technical specialists. These referral lists are typically provided as a searchable online database, accessed from the library's web portal. Librarians should make sure to get permission from these parties to be publicly noted. Librarians might also ask the school community for referrals to help build this human resource database. It should be noted, though, that individual names can be considered recommendations that librarians might be held accountable to, so it is usually better to cite agencies or directories rather than singling out individuals. Another good practice is to provide criteria for choosing experts, such as tips for selecting a tutor.

SELECTION PROCESSES

Thousands of reference sources exist, yet school libraries' budgets require careful selection of just a small percentage of available reference resources.

Selection Steps

School library reference collections exist to support the information needs of the school's community. Therefore, the first step in developing a reference collection is to conduct a needs assessment of that community. The most obvious source of data is the curriculum: syllabi, textbooks, reading lists, and class assignments, including sample student work. If the librarian has produced bibliographies or pathfinders, those documents can be reviewed by the subject teacher to determine their appropriateness. The librarian should also review the reference needs of special programs and co-curricular offerings such as clubs and after-school activities. Professional and parental reference needs and suggestions should also be considered. Focus groups with teachers and students can also provide valuable input about references that are used and unmet reference information needs; both frequent and infrequent library users should participate. The librarian should also look at the local community. Specifically, what other libraries can provide physical or digital access to reference sources to the school community? To what extent are these libraries used by the school community? Perhaps libraries can develop policies and procedures to share reference resources and services.

Next, the librarian should evaluate the existing current reference collection, primarily in terms of the curriculum and other reference needs of the school community rather than by Dewey Decimal Classification number. Because reference collections tend to be used in-house, reserves and reshelving trends are more illuminating than circulation records. As much as possible, the librarian should study online hits of library digital resources and open access search engine results to ascertain information-searching patterns. Most aggregator database services incorporate statistical data to ascertain use. If librarians keep records of reference questions, the results can also be used to identify reference needs, both in terms of references used as well as unanswered questions. Here are some guiding criteria:

- total number of reference titles and total by format;
- percentage of the total collection that is deemed reference;
- volume by curricular area, noting format;
- average age of titles by curricular area;
- general physical condition of titles by curricular area;
- balance of general, cross-curricular titles and subject-specific titles;
- most recent encyclopedias and atlases;

- non-English and mutlicultural references sources;
- online reference "monographs";
- aggregrator databases;
- percentage of titles that should be weeded by curricular area;
- strengths and weaknesses of the reference collection.

The more knowledgeable the librarian is about the school community and existing available resources, the more capable the librarian can be in keeping current about new reference publications that might be useful acquisitions.

Selection Tools

Nothing beats hands-on review of reference sources, especially if those items are also examined by relevant subject teachers. Some school districts and library systems have a central reviewing office or service. However, most school librarians need to rely on professional reviews, particularly those written by expert school librarians. Catalogs and bookstores are not strictly objective since vendors are in the business of selling. Here is a starting list of useful professional reference resource selection tools. In some cases, the entire source focuses on reference titles, but in most cases, reference recommendations constitute one section of the entire source. Dates are not indicated because most of these tools are updated frequently. It should be noted, though, that reference sources tend to stay stable; that is, you can expect the same kind of content and format year after year in a specific encyclopedia or reference guide, for instance. Several of these resources are available online and in print.

- *American Reference Books Annual*. Libraries Unlimited
- *Books for You: An Annotated Bibliography for Senior High Students*. National Council of Teachers of English.
- Children's Core Collection. Middle & Junior High Core Collection. Senior High Core Collection. H. W. Wilson.
- *Reference Books Bulletin*. American Library Association.
- *Core Collection for Children and Young Adults*. Scarecrow Press
- *Guide to Reference Books*. American Library Association
- *The Horn Book Guide to Children's and Young Adult Books*. McGraw-Hill
- *Recommended Reference Books for Small and Medium-Sized Libraries and Media Centers*. Libraries Unlimited
- New York Public Library's lists

Journals (* = sources that are the most central ones for school settings): *Booklist*, Choice, *Library Journal*, *Library Media Connection*, New York

*Review of Books, New York Times Book Review, Reference and Research Books News, The Reference Librarian, Reference Services Review, *School Library Journal,* and *Teacher Librarian.*

REFERENCE SOURCES LIFE CYCLE

Selecting reference materials is only the first step in reference collection development. This chapter has addressed several decisions and processes along the resource life cycle. Librarians need to develop policies and procedures to streamline and standardize practice.

Acquisition. Librarians need to maintain purchase order and inventory records.

Processing. How will resources be classified and cataloged? Will digital resources be cataloged? At the least, digital resources should be accessible through the library's web portal. As with other print materials, reference books need to be marked and labeled for easy identification and retrieval (e.g., a red stripe or REF label). Reference materials must stand up to heavy usage, so preventative measures such as reinforced spine and corner protection should be done. Dust jackets also provide protection.

Organization. How are materials organized and arranged in the library? Might some references be located outside the library facility? How will other resources be arranged: alphabetically, by subject matter, by format?

Circulation. Can reference materials circulate? Who can borrow them? What should be the borrowing period—and should it be differentiated by type of user (e.g., teachers)?

Maintenance. As with other print items, reference materials need to be kept in good physical condition so that they stay attractive and usable. To that end, library workers should peruse reference shelves regularly to look for spine damages and other signs of wear so repairs can be made quickly.

Deselection. The same criteria exist for reference withdrawals as for the rest of the collection: wear and other physical deterioration, outdated information, newer replacement editions, lack of use, lack of relevance. Occasionally, a worn volume is worth rebinding if no other copy or similar resource can replace it; usually, digitizing the volume is not cost-effective for school libraries. Librarians should keep an eye on reviews of new reference editions to find out if enough changes warrant replacement; sometimes it makes more sense to buy a different resource that covers approximately the same content. Johnson (2009) suggested some weeding time frames for specific types of references:

- almanacs: yearly;
- encyclopedias: five years;

- atlases: five years;
- dictionaries: five to ten years (depending on the subject).

In those cases where the information is still accurate, such as an almanac, the item that is replaced by the newest edition may be reassigned to the general collection or given to a teacher for classroom use. In the latter situation, the volume needs to be formally withdrawn from the library catalog inventory, with all library markings removed if possible. On the other hand, reference materials that are removed because of inaccuracies (e.g., new countries) should not be given to others; such practices would result in misinformation perpetuated by the library.

CORE REFERENCE COLLECTION SUGGESTIONS

Here are starting checklists of popular core reference titles, which are likely to be useful for most school settings.

Elementary

American Heritage First Dictionary and *Children's Dictionary*
Merriam-Webster's Elementary Dictionary and Visual Dictionary
Grolier Encyclopedia
World Book
New Book of Knowledge
New Children's Encyclopedia
Britannica Student Atlas
National Geographic Kids Animal Atlas
National Geographic Kids Almanac
Guinness World Records
Painless Junior Grammar and *Writing*
Usborne Introduction to Art
http://kids.usa.gov/
http://www.factmonster.com
http://www.refdesk.com/kids.html
http://www.kidsclick.org

Middle School

American Heritage Student Dictionary
Britannica Student Encyclopedia
National Geographic World Atlas for Young Explorers and *Student United States for Young Explorers*
Time for Kids Almanac

World Almanac for Kids
Kingfisher Illustrated Pocket Thesaurus
Greek and Roman Mythology
Lands and People
National Geographic Encyclopedia of Animals
Student's Guide to the U.S. Government Series
http://www.infoplease.com
http://www.sldirectory.com/virtual.html

High School: Winners

Merriam-Webster's Collegiate Dictionary
Merriam-Wester's Collegiate Thesaurus
Oxford Visual Dictionary
Encyclopedia Americana
Time Almanac
World Almanac
Statistical Abstract of the United States
Oxford Atlas of the World
Times Comprehensive Atlas of the World
Rand McNally Road Atlas
Shepherd's Historical Atlas
Columbia Gazetter of the World
Bartlett's Familiar Quotations
American Presidency (Encyclopedia Britannica)
Current Biography
American Decades (Gale)
Encyclopedia of World Religions
Harvard Dictionary of Music
Collins Dictionary of Literacy Terms
Gale Encyclopedia of Science
McGraw-Hill Encyclopedia of Science and Technology
McGraw-Hill Encyclopedia of World Biography
CRC Handbook of Chemistry and Physics
Atlas of the Human Body
Merck Manual
Culturegrams
Occupational Outlook Handbook
College Handbook
Opposing Viewpoints
Sports: The Complete Visual Reference
Rules of the Game
Writers Reference Center

Student Research Center (EBSCO)
Literature Resource Centers (Gale)
http://www.usa.gov
http://www.copyright.gov
http://www.cia.gov
http://www.usgovernmentmanual.gov
http://loc.gov
http://thomas.loc.gov
http://www.un.org/en/documents
http://data.un.org
http://www.credoreference.com
http://www.edmunds.com
http://www.bartleby.com
http://maps.google.com
http://www.biography.com
http://www.imdb.com
http://scienceworld.wolfram.com/biography
http://www.rhymezone.com
http://www.ipl.org/div/teen
http://www.reference.com
http://www.ala.org/rusa/sections/mars/marspubs/marsbestfreewebsites

High School: Runners-up

Acryonyms, Initialisms, and Abbreviations Dictionary
American National Biography
Chase's Calendar of Events
Chronology of World History
Consumer Reports
Emily Post's Etiquette
Encyclopedia of American Facts and Dates
Encyclopedia of Associations
Encyclopedia of World History
Granger's Index to Poetry
Grzimeck's Animal Life Encyclopedia
Masterplots
New Partridge Dictionary of Slang and Unconventional English
Oxford Dictionary of Art
Robert's Rules of Order
SIRS Researcher
Teen Health and Wellness
Timetables of History

Foreign language dictionary publishers: HarperCollins, Larousse, Oxford
    University Press

Professional

Sear's List of Subject Headings
Abridged Dewey Decimal Classification
http://www.worldcat.org
http://www.ala.org/ala/mgrps/divs/aasl/guidelinesandstandards/
    learningstandards/standards.cfm
http://www.libraryspot.com/
http://www.sldirectory.com/
http://www.kn.att.com/wired/fil/pages/listschoollma1.html
http://teachers.redclay.k12.de.us/mary.tise/liblinks.html

RESOURCE SHARING

Reference sources can be expensive. Libraries can leverage their budgets by
acquiring and sharing materials collectively. For instance, most states pay for
at least one aggregator database to be accessed by public school libraries.
School districts and library systems (both single and multitype) do joint
purchase orders as a way to get deep discounts on print and digital resource
materials. In addition, some school libraries within a district, or within close
geographic proximity, collectively do reference collection development and
divide reference areas by curriculum specialty among the sites so that one
school might focus on the arts and another might concentrate on science-
specific reference materials.

    When an information need cannot be fulfilled at one site, the library staff
can contact the site with the deeper reference collection to get the information. With scanners and faxes, this service can be an effective alternative to
purchasing a seldom-used reference volume. Materials might even by loaned
between sites. Of course, copyright needs to be observed; if an item is required multiple times, that is probably a good indication that the borrowing
library needs to acquire their own copy of the resource. A joint index of
reference sources, or simply the use of online catalogs, helps librarians keep
track of other sites' holdings, though it is good professional practice to notify
participating libraries about new acquisitions, so they can be better informed
when making their own purchasing decisions.

REFERENCES

Johnson, P. (2009). *Fundamentals of collection development and management* (2nd ed.). Chi-
    cago: American Library Association.

Levine-Clark, M., & Carter, T. (Eds.). (2013). *ALA glossary of library and information science* (4th ed.). Chicago: American Library Association.

Top 10 Reference Sources of the Century. (1999). *Library Journal, 124*(19), 34–38.

Chapter Five

Providing Physical Access

In order to use reference information, the school community needs to have physical access to it. In today's digital world, the options—and issues—are greatly expanded. Traditional questions of separate vs. integrated shelving have resurfaced, especially in light of bookstore influence. Several questions arise with reference resources: What should be cataloged—and to what extent? How can catalogs access specific information within resources? What cataloging programs and add-ons can enhance reference and information services? How can resources be accessed remotely, yet securely? How can guides to resource use be provided and linked? How can physical access be made to comply with the Americans with Disabilities Act? Physical access should facilitate both intentional and serendipitous retrieval.

CATALOGING AND ORGANIZATION

Reference materials gain their value in their use. Thus, they need to be readily and easily retrieved. In terms of access to physical resources, this involves both their carefully documented description and their physical arrangement within the collection.

To an extent, the school librarian needs to conceptualize how the reference resources will be arranged within the collection at the same time as determining how to catalog and label these items. The term "reference" is not cut-and-dried but rather may reflect the community's use of resources. Reference materials may be considered to represent a spectrum of resources ranging from comprehensive dictionaries and encyclopedias to art books and guides to literature. What may constitute a reference source for one course, such as a flower field guide, might serve as a general resource otherwise. Thus, most school librarians now label as reference only those materials that are generally considered "ready reference," such as those general dictionaries and encyclopedias noted above as well as comprehensive atlases, statistical resources, almanacs, handbooks, and directories. Other materials that might have mixed use—both as a quick reference and as more cover-to-cover use—are now usually interfiled with the general collection.

It should also be noted that reference material placement is also impacted by students' developmental level. Usually the quantity of reference materials grows along with the academic level. Nevertheless, books might be placed in an elementary school's reference section because they might require more adult guidance, such as health books. If the library does not have a separate parent or professional collection, some of those items might be placed in the elementary reference collection as well for quick retrieval. As with other library issues, determining the status and location of reference materials requires professional acuity and sensitivity to the community's needs.

The catalog should mirror the physical setup. For those items that are clearly identified as reference, the catalog would have a designation of REF (reference) in the call number, which is usually indicated in the MARC 852 field for holdings information ($k call number prefix). Typically those items are also located in a separate physical section. Many librarians place those volumes near their desk or the circulation desk so that the school community will associate those resources with getting quick information: from either a physical item or the information professional. It is usually a good idea to use 42-28" high shelving so individuals can consult the volume immediately by placing it on top of the range.

For those resources that situationally serve as reference sources, a reserve set of shelves—and temporary labels—can serve the purpose. These short-term reference materials usually have limited circulation rights in order to ensure that students can consult them throughout the day. In terms of the integrated library management system, the easiest way to address these items is through the materials type designation, which is normally linked to circulation rights. Usually material types are associated with classification numbers so that if students are doing a report on planets, then the Dewey Decimal Classification number 523.4 could be made a separate material type (which will then be applied to all of the planet resources with that number).

Regardless of the physical location, any item that might be considered to be on the reference "spectrum" should be thoroughly cataloged in order to facilitate its retrieval and use, particularly for high school collections. Thus, features such as bibliographies and indexes, maps, charts, and tables should be noted. Here are some applicable MARC fields to consider using:

300: Illustrative matter
490: Series statement

500: General notes, such as the index, and description of the nature and scope of the item

504: Bibliography

505: Formatted contents notes (e.g., tables of content)

520: Summary

526: Curriculum-based study

590: Local notes

While making decisions about physical access, school librarians also need to consider the needs of individuals with physical disabilities or limitations. At least one catalog station should provide for adjustable height to accommodate users in wheel chairs. Aisles should be at least 36" wide. Signage at the end of the ranges should be in LARGE type, preferably in raised letters. The library should provide some kind of scanner so that materials can be accessible for users with vision impairments; even a regular computer scanner with OCR (Optical Character Recognition) software can be used in conjunction with the computer's built-in text-to-speech program or more sophisticated installed software, such as Jaws. Fortunately, many reference materials are available digitally so they can be accessed without that intermediate scanning step.

School librarians also need to consider the social aspects of access. Students are often asked to do group projects, so the library needs to provide group working spaces so students can examine materials together. This joint access is particularly important with regard to physical access of digital resources. Even in the face of one computer per child, children work together online. Therefore, each computer station should have enough table surface to accommodate two chairs and school supplies of two students (Meyers, Fisher, & Marcoux, 2009).

DIGITAL REFERENCE RESOURCE ACCESS

As noted above, school libraries are increasingly offering digital reference resources. At one point in time, reference vendors offered CD-ROM versions of some of their products, particularly encyclopedias. Nowadays, these digital resources are usually stored remotely in the "cloud" to facilitate access from any Internet-connected computer. Even if the product license is limited to static IP addresses (site-based or even library-based), the librarian usually does not have to worry about physical product installation or updating. Normally, licenses enable several individuals to access the product simultaneously, which was harder to do with CD-ROMs, even if they were loaded onto the library or school server.

Increasingly, school librarians aim for school community access to reference materials from school, home, or other remote site. This option is possible with dynamic IP addresses in conjunction with log-in and password procedures to authorize and authenticate eligible users. A good practice is to establish one log-in and password for all library digital reference products, if possible; that option may depend on the vendors' own setup requirements. In any case, the log-in and password can be made available on library posters and handouts (such as bookmarks) and in the school newsletter. Librarians should *not* provide the log-in/password on the library portal; that information invites strangers to use the digital products, and the librarian could find himself or herself liable for contract agreement infringement. Especially if the license limits the number of simultaneous users, outsiders could well preempt rightful users from accessing the needed information.

A library portal offers the most convenient and efficient way to provide access to digital reference sources. At the least, the integrated library management system (ILMS) can serve that purpose. Today's ILMSs have the capacity to provide the links to the product, not just the bibliographical information. For instance, Follett's Destiny program has the flexibility of providing a separate menu for digital resources or combining all types of resources into one search field. Additionally, most ILMS vendors provide mobile app access. Typically, aggregator databases are handled similarly to a periodical, with the advantage of being linked to the database from the basic catalog and then searching within that database. Parsing reference e-books from other e-books is more problematic, but is solved with a searchable REF call number field designation. Some university libraries with high-end ILMSs now provide the capacity for truly one-stop access for users; their keywords generate entries *within* individual aggregrator databases so that the user doesn't even have to decide which database to access. On the other hand, when students type in "Saturn," they may end up with fifty thousand entries for all sorts of resources, resembling an overwhelming Google search.

Aggregator databases, as seen above, can pose access challenges for both the librarian and user. Most states in the United States pay for public and school library database subscriptions for at least a couple of aggregator databases such as Academic Search or eLibrary. These databases then are likely to be accessed via the state's portal, so the local library has to set up the protocols for log-in and linkage to the appropriate website. School districts may pay for database subscriptions across schools, so the same site-based issue of linkages has to be addressed; this problem is often sidestepped because these same districts are likely to provide a district union ILMS that incorporates the database access protocol. Nevertheless, even if these other sources of database subscriptions exist, a school library might still subscribe to a unique aggregator database. If possible, all the databases should be accessed from one web page since the end user usually does not care where the database resides but just wants access to the specific information. Since a file or URL can be linked from several places within a website, librarians should err on the side of providing several access points as appropriate. If school librarians want to emphasize the reference collection, they can include a link from the library portal home page to a reference web page with the list of options: aggregator databases, reference physical and e-books, and reference websites or directories.

It should be noted that students do like federated searching, that is, a one-stop search "box" that can search across databases. Sometimes libraries will subscribe to several aggregator databases but opt for different levels of access depending on the database. This situation arises because major vendors, or a vendor with several products, might have considerable resource overlap; because vendors tend to offer a package of resources rather than letting the library choose individual titles, the library may end up with a couple of aggregator databases from competing vendors that include the same sources. Rather than paying twice for the same periodical article, the librarian might subscribe to the full-text version of one major aggregator database and the citation-only version of another overlapping aggregator database. Open URL link resolvers interface with these databases, enabling the user to access the targeted resource from any of the databases subscribed to; SFX is the most widely used link resolver, which is fee-based. School libraries tend to subscribe to just a handful of aggregator databases, so this option is usually not used. Nevertheless, as ILMSs become more sophisticated, it is useful for librarians to keep abreast of such developments.

Website-specific reference resources demand separate attention in terms of access. Traditionally, school libraries have provided a web page directory of linked reference websites, usually arranged by curricular subject. This practice reflects the concept of information organization by format. Some school librarians catalog websites as they would other resources. Alternatively, librarians can create their own customized search engines that include a list of library-identified reference websites from which to choose; the most popular generator is Google Custom Search Engine. This approach enables students to search across websites, much like other search engines, but be limited to curriculum-relevant and developmentally appropriate resources. While major reference-centric websites tend to have stable URLs, librarians still need to check them periodically to avoid broken links; this task sometimes can be delegated to library aides. Another option is to provide links to a few existing library reference directories, which lessens the maintenance burden. Representative reference directories follow, which are best used in high school libraries.

- American Library Association: http://gws.ala.org/category/reference-desk
- Library of Congress Virtual Reference Shelf: http://www.loc.gov/rr/askalib/virtualref.html

- Internet Public Library: http://www.ipl.org/IPLBrowse/GetSubject?vid= 13&tid=6996&parent=0
- Internet Library for Librarians: http://www.itcompany.com/inforetriever/ index.htm
- Michigan State University: http://staff.lib.msu.edu/sowards/home/home2. htm
- Breitlinks: http://www.breitlinks.com/my_libmedia/online_ready_ reference.htm
- Kids Click: http://www.kidsclick.org/topfact.php
- Kid Info: http://www.kidinfo.com/School_Subjects.html
- Fact Monster: http://www.factmonster.com/

THE BIG PICTURE ABOUT LIBRARY PORTALS

Nowadays most school libraries have a library portal, which acts as an ongoing, organized introduction to the school library program of resources and services. The library portal also extends access to the library program beyond the four walls of the library and the school's operating hours. Even if the ILMS and databases can be accessed only at the school site, the library portal can provide access to generally available relevant reference sources as well as offer information service in the form of research guides.

Most school library portals include the following information:

- library location, hours, and staff contact information;
- library services and procedures;
- link to the library catalog (which sometimes serves as the library portal);
- links to library databases;
- links to other libraries;
- library news.

Other features include: bibliographies and pathfinders such as LibGuides, new acquisitions, reviews, RIS blogs or wikis, citation style help, research guidance, reference help, web tutorials, Internet safety tips, library contests, RIS widgets (e.g., fact of the day, weather, the day's newspaper), class visit scheduling calendar, RIS video or webinar archives, and links with the rest of the school. The portal should also showcase the librarian's instructional role: through research guidance, reference help, and web tutorials. In addition, the library portal should provide the school community ways to participate and contribute to the library portal, such as website recommendations and sample student work.

School library portals may include instant messaging widgets to provide synchronous RIS or at least links to online digital reference services. School librarians should also consider incorporating Skype or web conferencing options in order to provide a richer RIS experience to classrooms at point of need. Whiteboard features can enable the librarian to give presentations and demonstrate useful websites. With shared screens, other parties can demonstrate information use for the librarian to coach and guide. With a webcam, librarians can show actual pages from reference sources, and users can show their information issue for the librarian to help solve. This interactive instructional approach enables school librarians to virtually access the rest of the school site and extend their instructional role when it is most needed.

Even with the best resources and participatory potential, the library portal may be ignored if it is not well designed. The overall appearance of the library portal should reflect the philosophy and approach of the library. For instance, an elementary school library portal might have bright colors and sans serif font, use simple vocabulary, provide family-friendly websites and videos, and include a parent web page. On the other hand, a high school library can look more sophisticated to convey a college-prep attitude or use teen-generated graphics to invite student participation. High school library portals might have separate web pages for academic department-specific RIS as well as a career/college web page and a web page for co-curricula and teen issues. In fact, some school library portals are designed by students themselves. In any case, it's a good idea to have students pilot-test and review the library's portal to make sure it is clear, useful, and engaging. Some criteria to use in evaluating the library portal include:

- Content: Is all content accurate, relevant, and developmentally appropriate? Does the portal provide an accurate, engaging sense of the library's program and the use of the library web portal? Are all digital resources described adequately?
- Layout: Does the home page attract and engage the user? Are the web pages clear and organized? Doe the order of the web pages seem logical? Do visual elements and text work well together effectively and aesthetically? Do pages have a consistent look to facilitate finding the needed information?
- Navigation: Does a navigation bar guide the user to the relevant pages? Is it easy and logical to go from one page to another? Is it easy to keep track of consulted pages? Is there a help feature?
- Text: Is the text easy to read and comprehend? Is the writing engaging? Is the writing free of mechanical errors? Is the vocabulary developmentally appropriate? Is font use appropriate and consistent?
- Technical aspects: Do all technical elements work properly in all browsers? Does the site make good use of hyperlinks? Do all links work? Do multimedia resources work properly?

- Accessibility: Does the library portal comply with Americans with Disabililities Act website standards?

The website http://schoollibrarywebsites.wikispaces.com/ provides ideas for impactful school library websites. AASL's list of best websites for teaching and learning, http://www.ala.org/aasl/standards-guidelines/best-websites, also offers good website criteria as well as useful resources.

It should be remembered that the most important aspect of the library portal is information, so a clean, organized look without lots of graphics should be the goal. Especially since some families may have dial-up Internet access or use mobile devices to access the library portal, images should be kept to a minimum. A solid light-colored background can serve as the visual attraction. In fact, school librarians should ask ILMS and database vendors for mobile-friendly versions, and they should also make sure that products comply with the Americans with Disabililities Act (ADA). For that reason, website frames and tables should be avoided, and all images need alternative text. Several websites can check for ADA compliance. The following websites provide valuable advice:

- http://www.usability.gov/how-to-and-tools/index.html
- http://www.ala.org/ascla/asclaprotools/accessibilitytipsheets
- http://www.w3.org/WAI/gettingstarted/, especially the section on evaluating accessibility

THE MERITS OF BROWSING

Fortunately, most school libraries are open access. However, even then the reference section often gets lost in the shuffle. This phenomenon happens for several reasons: poor signage, location (such as trapped between other sections or tucked behind the circulation desk), physical appearance (e.g., overwhelming tomes, drab covers, older copyright), and lack of explicit publicity about them.

When reference collections include a wide spectrum of titles, they might be used more, but the impact of the titles themselves might get diffused—or seem confusing. Especially if the reference collection does not circulate, students may end up having less access to materials in the long run. On the other hand, a streamlined reference collection might lend itself to more quick queries but might also suffer being overlooked if other reference-like materials are in the general collection; students tend to like one-stop searching.

Once the reference collection is visible and known, it's more likely to be browsed. Indeed, browsing is a good habit to reinforce because it helps users broaden their perspective and link concepts together. In that respect, both arrangements of reference materials—enclusive and narrowly defined sections—have advantages: a smaller reference collection can lead to more cross-disciplinary browsing and greater crossover between reference materials and other titles in the general part of the collection, while a big reference collection highlights the range of reference materials and optimizes the availability of reference titles in any given subject. Fortunately, the Dewey Decimal Classification system, which most school libraries employ, also reinforces browsing habits because similar topics are likely to be close to each other. Shelf-specific labels, such as "science" or "biographies" can also facilitate quick perusal when browsing.

Rice, McGreadie, and Chang (2001) developed a framework of library browsing habits. They identified four influences: physical movement, motivational purpose, cognitive knowledge, and resource focus. Individuals might be in the library and just start looking around. Sometimes they have a specific information need or want to keep current on a topic (such as sports), and other times they are responding to an invitation to browse. As a result of browsing, these individuals may accidentally or purposefully find an interesting resource, they satisfy their curiosity, they learn something, they get updated, and they may feel more relaxed.

In any case, browsing the reference shelves alerts users to materials that they might have never considered before. Particularly since bookstores tend to sell just the most popular ready-reference titles such as dictionaries and almanacs, students might not know about standard titles found in libraries, which constitute the main market for reference publishers. Multivolume sets, such as *The McGraw-Hill Encyclopedia of World Biography* or *American Decades*, are especially rare outside of libraries. While many youngsters cut their reference teeth on the *Guinness Book of World Records*, few of them discover treasures such as moon atlases or picture chronologies if they are not encouraged to browse reference shelves. From upper elementary grades on up, reference browsing can be a fun and fruitful adventure.

It should be noted that online reference browsing can also be an addictive activity. For that reason, digital reference titles should be cataloged or somehow featured so that users will be able to browse through them easily. Databases constitute an often overlooked aspect of library portals when it comes to browsing, which is a shame since several products are very compelling, such as CultureGrams, Discover streaming, and PressDisplay. Even highlighting one online reference source per week in the library portal can lead to repeat online-reference-browsing business.

REFERENCES

Meyers, E., Fisher, K., & Marcoux, E. (2009). Making sense of an information world: The everyday-life information behavior of preteens. *Library Quarterly, 79*(3), 301–341.

Rice, R., McCreadie, M., & Chang, S. (2001). *Accessing and browsing: Information and communication.* Cambridge, MA: MIT Press.

Chapter Six

Conducting Reference Interactions

The traditional core of reference service was the reference interview. Other terms are replacing that concept, such as conversation and interaction, in order to emphasize the process as a negotiated and partnership model. Both synchronous and asynchronous options are addressed, such as video conferencing to classrooms. Specific guidelines and techniques are then suggested, including ways to help individuals with special needs. Consortium and outsourced digital reference services are also examined. It is also noted that informal just-in-time help can be equally effective; walk-around reference help is increasingly recommended.

STANDARDS

The American Association of School Librarians (2009) stated that school librarians need to carry out the roles of information specialist, instructional partner, teacher, program administrator, and leader. Their standards are couched in terms of expected actions: teaching for learning, building the learning environment, and empowering learning through leadership.

Reference Service Standards

More specifically, the Reference and User Services Association (RUSA) developed standards for RIS (http://www.ala.org/rusa/resources/guidelines), which includes collection development, electronic services, behavior performances, professional competencies, and services for specific populations. In explaining the professional competencies, the RUSA task force (2003) focused on unique RIS competencies behind the overall professional competencies of literacy, communication, and general library science knowledge. The RIS competencies are clustered as follows:

- Access: responsiveness to user needs, organization and design of services to meet community needs, and critical thinking and analysis of information sources and services.
- Knowledge base: structure of information resources, influence of technology on the structure of informatiom, basic information tools, information behaviors of users, interactive communication principles, intellectual property law, and information competency standards.
- Knowledge strategies: environmental scanning, assessment techniques, knowledge application to improve RIS, dissemination of knowledge, active learning.
- Marketing/Awareness/Informing: conducting research and assessment about appropriate RIS and potential users, communication and outreach about existing RIS, evaluation of marketing efforts.
- Collaboration: perception of user as information-seeking collaborator; collaboration with colleagues, other information professionals, and others to provide RIS.
- RIS assessment: surveying users and their information needs, assessing RIS effectiveness, matching users' capabilities and service technology requirements, assessing information interfaces, evaluating RIS staff performance.

Understanding the difference between content knowledge and communication skills, the Reference and User Services Association (2013) developed guidelines for behavioral performance of RIS providers irrespective of the interactive space (i.e., face-to-face or remote), as follows.

- Visibility and approachability: easy to find, able to make user comfortable, begins interaction in a timely manner.
- Interest: shows interest through focused attention and maintains voice contact.
- Listening and inquiring: can identify user's needs through an appropriate communication tone, clarifies the request, using open-ended and closed questions, while maintaining objectivity and respecting the user.
- Searching: constructs a complete, time-sensitive, competent search strategy by building on and collaborating with user's efforts, instructing and guiding the user on search strategies and use.
- Follow-up: determines the need for additional information or referrals, consulting with other experts as needed, making the user aware of other information sources.

Youth-Specific Standards

The Reference and User Services Association (2007) also developed guidelines to address the unique information interests and needs of teenagers. Because teens like to experiment or may be curious about adult issues, librarians need to deal respectfully and sensitively with possible questions regarding sexuality, drug use, self-mutilation, cults, or extreme practices. In addition, since many of their requests rise from questions imposed by classroom teachers, librarians also have to wade through the filter of youth not understanding the assignment—or teachers not being clear. These imposed information tasks may make the student feel powerless, and they may resent being put into a situation where they have to ask for help, thus demonstrating even less power or control. Therefore, whenever possible, librarians should interact with the associated teachers so that the information request can be dealt with directly. Particularly since students assume that the librarian and teacher work together, knowing the assignment ahead of time can help the librarian serve as a knowledgeable coach and co-searcher with the student.

Not only do youth's queries demand special attention, but youth's developmental issues also require careful attention. As noted elsewhere, a central aspect of youth is their physical development: in terms of cognition, psychology, and physiology. For instance, formal logic might not be well developed until high school years, and their sense of morality and consequences are also in developmental stages during the teenage years. Youth's expectations of themselves and others may also be inaccurate; their sense of the length of time needed to conduct research can be short-sided, they may over- or underestimate their ability to find information, and they may lack patience to persevere in their research effort. The resultant RUSA guidelines for teens take these realities into consideration.

- Integrate RIS for youth into the library's plan and RIS program, which may require additional funding and facilities.
- Exhibit friendly, positive, courteous, and objective professional service during each interaction. It is especially important to respect youth's privacy and sense of fairness.
- Use current information and communication technology resources and services, including social media, to address youth's information needs. Understand how youth perceive and interact with the world using technologies.
- Provide information and informational resources that address youth's academic and personal informational needs. Involve them in reference collection development.

- Provide RIS that is developmentally appropriate. Incorporate instruction and learning activities that help them gain information literacy. Encourage youth to help plan and implement RIS.
- Partner with youth-serving agencies and groups to optimize RIS.

Youth have their own assumptions about library RIS. They consider it as an academic safety net where they can get needed facts and resources. Here are some of their school library RIS standards, or at least expectations:

- friendly atmosphere, be it face-to-face or online;
- close collaboration between classroom teacher and librarian;
- guidance and coaching;
- selected websites;
- easy and convenient: "Just the facts."

The more that school librarians know how youth "tick" and understand their worlds (e.g., gaming, anime, social activities), the more likely that they can understand teens' information needs. Librarians need to respect students and develop trustworthy relationships. In addition, demonstrating care and acknowledging teens' emotional needs also positively impact RIS interaction.

THE PHYSICAL AND VIRTUAL CONTEXT OF REFERENCE INTERACTION

The physical context of the reference interaction significantly impacts the process and results. This issue reinforces the adage that actions can speak louder than words. For instance, when a librarian stands with arms closed behind a tall counter and stares down at an elementary student, the ensuing reference interaction will likely fail. Students can feel intimidated or inconsequential in such situations. Instead the underlying principle is to aim for equal footing and comfort. Here are some tips.

- Aim for equal height to optimize eye contact, which is easiest to achieve by having both parties sit.
- Match body language (e.g., arm gestures, posture).
- Try to remove any physical barriers between yourself and the user. If there's a reference desk, place the chair on the side of the desk so the two parties are seated at right angles to each other. If the furniture location permits, set the chairs on the same side or use a bench instead of chairs.
- Mount the computer screen on a swingable arm to facilitate joint viewing. Use a wireless keyboard or one with a long cable to enable the student to use it.

- Change the look of the desk. Make it more welcoming and attractive. Personalize it. Brighten it up. Downsize it. Transform the reference desk into a genius bar or round café-type table with stools.
- Train students to answer information needs, such as catalog use, database use, and productivity program use. Have them manage the genius bar.
- Go to the point of user need. Rove the library, and observe students who look "stuck" or frustrated. Some cues include: off-task behavior, staring for minutes at a computer monitor without any other body movement, stressful or sad expression or other body language. Then offer to help.
- Visit classes and introduce yourself—or have the teacher introduce you. Provide RIS at their point of need.
- Provide class reference service virtually through voice-over-IP (e.g., Skype) or web conferencing channel.

The location of the RIS desk itself conveys a message about service. In smaller libraries there may be only one desk, which serves as the circulation and information service center. Even in such small quarters, it's good to have a separate checkout station so that circulation records are kept confidential. Logically, the RIS "center" should be located near the reference collection and research computers. Increasingly, libraries are using movable desks or tables for at-point-of-need information services. While mobility can be convenient, it also creates a sense of unpredictability, which can confuse students.

Labels and signage also contribute to the psychological aspect of RIS interaction. Some students might not understand the term "reference" and would be more familiar with the term "help desk." While students should learn library lingo to some extent, they should not have to guess where to get help. Signs and graphics also aid in making RIS more visible; here are some ideas.

- With students, brainstorm other terms beside reference desk: reference center, information center, answer desk, help desk, info central, brain bar, genius bar, Q/A desk, idea central.
- With students, brainstorm RIS slogans: "Here to help you," "Check us out," "Do you have questions? We have answers," "Work smarter," "Serving information," "Information connection," "Get answers here," "Free answers here," "Get smarter here."
- With students, brainstorm other terms besides reference or school librarian: information scientist, cybrarian, information navigator, info specialist, information connector, media specialist, library teacher, information professional.
- Hang a labeled banner, perhaps in the shape of an oversized arrow, above the RIS center.

- Put a name plate and function label on the desk (e.g., Mr. Jones, your Cybrarian).
- With students, brainstorm RIS logos and emoticons: question mark, inter-abang, the letter I, light bulbs, thumbs up (may be offensive in some cultures), raised index finger, open hand, shaking hands, upward arrow, lightning bolt, national library logo, UNESCO information literacy logo (http://www.ifla.org/publications/integrating-the-information-literacy-logo-a-marketing-manual).

INTERACTING WITH POPULATIONS WITH SPECIAL NEEDS

School librarians work with the entire school community and beyond as they provide RIS. Therefore, their practices should be as inclusive as possible. Interaction should exhibit behaviors that can be understood by the broadest audience possible; this approach is especially applicable for whole class presentations. Here are some general tips.

- Create a positive climate. Make learning safe and comfortable.
- Provide clear information and expectations.
- Help students to connect RIS to their own environments.
- Offer instruction or other kinds of support if students are not used to locating or using resources independently.
- Provide support and scaffolding for students as needed: online tutorials, local expertise, peer assistants, translation tools, technical help.
- Give students time to process and evaluate information. Foster critical thinking by modeling analytical information processing.
- Help students clarify and explain their understanding.
- Build fluency through practice.

The principles of universal design also apply well here: providing users with choices in how information is represented (e.g., format, language, reading level), in how they engage and interact with information (e.g., level of inter-est, amount of time, depth of information), and in how they demonstrate competence.

Language can be a major stumbling block in RIS. As much as possible, librarians should provide reference sources and help in a language that the student can understand. In some cases, a student may be able to comprehend English better orally or better in written form, so when one format does not work well, the librarian should try an alternative format. In that respect, asynchronous online RIS can be a good alternative for English learners be-cause they can have time to translate content with less time stress. In general, providing written and oral information simultaneously, and incorporating visual cues, is the best practice. It should be noted that some images may be unrecognizable or demeaning or have different meanings to different cultures. Sarkodie-Manash (2000) and Ferrer-Vinent (2010) offered several suggestions that apply well to English learners as well as other populations.

- In all interactions, use plain English and short sentences, and avoid idioms. Rephrase and simplify statements. Use meaningful gestures.
- Speak clearly and slowly without accent.
- Use repetition, paraphrasing, and summaries.
- Focus attention on essential vocabulary needed for RIS. Provide bilingual glossaries and visual references. Define new terms.
- Use visual aids and graphic organizers to help users understand content organization and relationships.
- Include frequent comprehension checks and clarification questions.
- If you can't understand the user, don't pretend to.
- If possible, instruct in the user's primary language (unless a group of users represent several native languages).
- Pair users linguistically.
- Maintain a list of world speakers. International students usually like to do follow-up questions in their primary language.
- Employ hands-on learning.

RIS can be especially problematic for immigrant teens because of first-country differences in practices and values. Not only might immigrants lack knowledge about libraries and their benefits, but they may also harbor negative attitudes toward government. Moreover, in some countries, reading is not considered very important. What with immigrant families focusing on survival and acculturation, education and technology usually take a back seat (Constantino, 1998). Schools should provide transition services for new immigrants, both students and their families, and such orientation should include the library. Ideally, public librarians and school librarians can co-present information about library services and procedures, including free library cards and borrowing privileges.

Students with disabilities represent a wide variety of issues: physical, cognitive, and psychological. Whenever possible, school librarians should consult with the student's teacher and other resource team members. Frequently, students with special needs have a peer buddy or adult aide to facilitate interaction. Nevertheless, the librarian should interact directly with the target student rather than ignoring that person. Several of the practices mentioned above for English language learners also apply well to students with disabilities. Some additional suggestions from Greene & Kochhar-Bryant (2003) follow.

- Break down directions into smaller steps.
- Interact in a consistent manner.
- Use concrete, literal terms.
- Minimize obstacles and distractions, such as background noise.
- Build on student interests.
- Take into account the affective side of interaction so that students remain positive and engaged.
- As noted for universal design, provide options for information, comprehension, communication, and action.

Most importantly, school librarians should remember that students with special needs are growing and unique individuals first. Showing interest, respect, and care provides the foundation for successful interaction in any case.

PURPOSEFUL RIS INTERACTION

While browsing the library collection, and the reference resources in particular, can result in wonderful serendipitous learning, most RIS interaction is initiated by the user who has an information query. Experienced school librarians know the school's curriculum, users' developmental needs and capacities, and typical contexts so that they can match the right information with the right person at the right time.

Types of Reference Questions

The nature of RIS interaction depends on the users' need and intent. For instance, providing a suggestion for a good thriller differs substantively from helping insert a video into a PowerPoint or developing a search strategy for a science fair project. Generally, reference questions fall into several categories. Each type of information need should be handled in specific ways.

Directional. Where is the copier? When is the library open? To handle these and similar information needs, the library should provide highly visible signage and handouts to deal with reccurring questions. A FAQ page can help online users with many of this type of question.

Material requests. Do you own a copy of *Charlotte's Web*? Is the field guide to birds on the shelf? The circulation desk usually handles these questions, and the online library catalog should include holdings information so that users can learn how to find out this information for themselves. A reference chart can also be placed by the OPAC stations to facilitate self-direction. While it is best for the librarian to walk with the user to the shelf to locate the desired item, distinctive signage and visual cues can help direct the user to the appropriate shelf if the librarian cannot leave the desk (e.g., "Go to the third shelf below the koala picture to find books about Australia").

Ready reference. Who is France's president? Where is Annapolis? To answer this type of query, the librarian should have a handful of core reference resources at hand: for example, an almanac, an atlas, a dictionary, an encyclopedia, a citation/stylebook, the school handbook. Most of these ready reference are also available online and should be bookmarked for quick retrieval—as well as featured on the library portal's reference page. Whenever possible, the librarian should verbalize the process of finding the fact so that the student can do it independently in the future. The librarian should also remind the student to note at least the source title, date, and page for the information found.

Procedural-based searches. How do I find an article in a database? How do I find statistical information? These requests can be dealt with at point-of-need, giving just enough information to accomplish that particular task. That approach may be all the directions that the user can handle at the moment. Even then, it's a good idea for the librarian to find out the context of the request, such as the student needing a primary source from the Civil War era or a dataset in order to make numerical predictions; such situational details help the librarian determine what process the student needs to learn.

Technology instruction. How do I double space? How do I download an article? Users assume that library staff know every piece of software and application on the library computers. As much as possible, library workers should become familiar with the main features of each program and practice using them. To cut down on time, one person can take the lead in knowing the program and then coach the other library workers. Workers, by the way, can include adult and student volunteers. At the least, a reference page should be available, in print and online format, as a "cheat sheet" to guide the novice user. If the query seems to involve a long, detailed training session, then the librarian should probably refer the user to an expert such as the school's computer teacher or technology specialist. Again, it is a good practice for the school, perhaps under the guidance of the librarian, to have a student tech squad who can serve as peer coaches in this capacity.

Standard and in-depth reference. How do I find information on the impact of slavery on the British Empire? What research has been done on water pollution in the local river? For those librarians who like research, these kinds of questions affirm the importance of library science academic preparation and help students become college-ready. These one-on-one or small group sessions involve an iterative series of queries about the topic and context, the user's current knowledge and skills, as well as instruction on search strategies, the use of specific resources, and processes in interpreting and manipulating information. Students can demonstratively see how reseach truly involves re-searching. These in-depth interactions can be difficult to do when a whole class is working in the library; if possible, scheduling a consultation provides the optimum environment for this interactive learning. However, even a five- to ten-minute conversation can offer a rich learning experience. Particularly when a class is doing I-Search papers, which involve metacognitive journaling while researching a self-chosen topic, the teacher can require each student to have a five-minute research consultation session with the librarian; the student can choose at what point to talk with the librarian, which puts the student in control and allows him or her to determine the point of need.

Other just-in-time help. What's the e-mail address for my teacher? I missed the bus—when is the next one coming? As noted elsewhere, the library often serves as the school's information safety net, the go-to place in a crisis. The librarian needs to know the resources and services of the school and community and be ready at any point to deal calmly with a panicked user's information needs.

Reader's Advisory

Reader's advisory constitutes a major function for school librarians. "What's another book series like *Hunger Games*?" "Do you have a picture book about turtles?" "I have to read a book for class that is at least two hundred pages long; do you have large-type books or long comics?" As reader's advisors, school librarians are personal advisors and social agents; they help users understand others and broaden their intellectual horizons (Dali, 2010). Especially as the school librarian gets to know the student and his or her reading habits over time, recommendations of good reads will be more relevant and fruitful. Librarians often ask readers what they like to read and may get a nondescript answer, such as "Anything," or librarians may ask about the last good book a student read, only to get the answer, "I don't remember." The best time to ask such a question is when the student is returning the book. It is usually more beneficial to ask about a students' interests, including their favorite TV or movies.

Reader's advisory can also be a comfort for students under stress, say from a divorce or family illness. Both nonfiction and fiction resources can be useful: for factual background information and for fictionalized insights into coping techniques. It should be noted, however, that librarians are seldom trained psychologists and so should be careful when considering bibliotherapy; it is usually a better idea to consult with the school psychologist about the student at risk.

In some schools, students keep reading logs, which can track their reading journey. While the librarian could store these reading logs, students will have a greater sense of responsibility and ownership if they keep their own logs, and they can consult those logs when they visit other libraries or bookstores. Nowadays, students can use moble reading log apps, and databases such as LibraryThing and Goodreads also offer app options.

Unlike the public librarian, who tends to focus on answering a user's information question by locating the resource or specific fact, the school librarian tries to leverage a reference interaction as a learning opportunity to instruct users. One of the attractive features of the school library is its user-centric approach. The school librarian models individualized, differentiated instruction. The reference interaction seeks to determine what the user wants or needs, and that person's current information literacy status, in order to figure out an effective way to meet that information need. Sometimes in these just-in-time reference instructional sessions, the librarian may refer to a reference sheet or presentation. However, the strength of the interaction is its personalization. More formal instructional strategies are covered in the next chapter.

Reference instruction can range from a stock orientation to the library catalog or basic database search protocols to complex individualized search strategies. In each case, school librarians try to describe the process and the rationale for each action so that the student can do it for him- or herself the next time. Increasingly, instruction involves technology tools; whenever possible, librarians should have the inquirer control the keyboard and mouse actions to ensure a hands-on experience.

WHAT IS THE REAL QUESTION?

Sometimes it is hard for the librarian to figure out the "real" information need of youth. Sometimes the question itself is the problem, and sometimes the student's own knowledge, behaviors, or dispositions can be the source of difficulty.

Imposed questions certainly raise issues. The question itself may be unclear or omit important information. Sometimes the teacher does not communicate well the question or information task. The student might not cognitively understand the question or have the academic background to address it adequately. Furthermore, the student might not be interested in the information task or think it worthwhile to pursue. While it is not the responsibility of librarians to mediate between teachers and students, and the librarian may even encounter resistance from the teacher for "interfering," librarians do have the responsibility of providing the highest caliber of RIS, and that includes optimizing the conditions for learning and student success. Therefore, if the student and librarian cannot successfully resolve the imposed question, the librarian should try not to second-guess the teacher but rather conduct the reference interaction with the original question poser. This interaction has the benefit of revealing the teacher's intent, expectation of students, anticipation of available resources, expectations of type and degree of library service and support, and expectation of the ultimate student product. This situation can be ameliorated if the librarian can have this reference conversation before the teacher assigns the information task, and it is even better if the librarian and teacher can collaboratively design the information task.

Sensitive topics also raises barriers. Imagine the student whispering to the librarian, "I need information about abortions," and the librarian asking for the student to repeat that louder. Imagine that librarian then loudly saying, "Oh, you must be doing the abortion report." Some students may be uncomfortable with that assigned topic in the first place, and in the second place the need may be personal or asked for on behalf of a relative or friend. If the librarian makes the wrong assumption, he or she might direct the student to the wrong information, along with embarrassing the student. Sometimes a student "disguises" such information queries by broadening the topic to "dating" or "human development," which can also result in irrelevant information. When possibly sensitive topics arise, the librarian needs to take extra care to discuss the information need in a confidential way. It also helps if the librarian can check with the probable teacher ahead of time in order to be alerted about such information tasks. For instance, if the health teacher is asking students to research topics about sexuality, the librarian can prepare print and digital pathfinders to help student self-locate appropriate information. A reference reserve shelf with useful resources can also facilitate self-help reference support.

Students may also have difficulty wording an information query, either in interacting with the librarian or in developing a string of search terms. Sometimes students have a limited vocabulary and do not know appropriate synonyms; librarians can show students how to find synonyms using print and online resources. Librarians can also explain to students how to use general reference tools such as encyclopedias to generate likely key terms. Students may also have difficulty determining the appropriate scope of their information task, either asking too broad of a question or too narrow of one. Again, encyclopedias can be consulted in order to demonstrate the value of headings and subheadings. Online directories also provide guidance in understanding how to define the scope of a topic; applicable websites include: http://www.clusty.com/, http://www.ipl.org/div/subject/, http://dir.yahoo.com/, and http://www.kidsclick.org/.

Students may also filter their own questions in anticipation of the librarian's response. They might not want to "bother" the librarian and so ask a general locational question such as "Where are the history books?" thinking that they can browse that part of the library in order to find a resource that answers their real need to find the causes of the Cold War. Sometimes a student will try to "talk library" by asking where the atlases are rather than ask the real question: "What was the geographic area of the Hapsburg Empire?" Librarians need to explain that RIS is a core service and that librarians welcome the opportunity to share in the process of discovering information, starting wherever the student is comfortable.

Other internal obstacles exist: language, mental processing differences, speech limitations, sensory impairments, mobility issues. In addition, students might have time constraints, lack of access to technology, and lack of opportunities for learning and practicing research skills. Sometimes a student might refuse to answer the librarian's question or may give a misleading answer. Sometimes when a referral is the most appropriate action, the student might not want to accept that solution because it involves transportation or an uncomfortable situation (e.g., fear of going to a medical library). All of these impact how students construct information questions and interact with the librarian (Ross, 1998).

Online RIS also impacts questioning. Most interaction is text-based, so the two parties do not have the luxury of experiencing and interpreting paralanguage such as speech patterns and body gestures. Typing itself can be laborious so that response rates can be slow and frustrating. While the librarian is searching for relevant resources, he or she should try to communicate the searching and decision-making process so the student doesn't feel isolated or abandoned. On the other hand, online RIS can facilitate question construction because some students find it easier to type than to speak, or at least less intimating. English learners can instantly translate the librarian's conversation using digital translation tools or translate their own questions in another question into English for the librarian to understand. Students also feel more anonymous online, and so may ask a more direct question, especially on a sensitive topic, than they would face-to-face. Unfortunately, that anonymity can backfire in that the online reference librarian usually cannot tell the age or intent of the questioner. Online reference service is seldom conducted by a school librarian, and most other librarians do not know the school's curriculum or likely assignments. Consequently, the online reference librarian might not use developmentally appropriate wording or provide appropriate guidance. On their part, students assume that the online librarian is local and knows the school community and class assignments, so assumptions and misunderstandings arise—as does frustration. Ideally, school librarians should provide online reference service to optimize the reference interaction and support.

In all cases, librarians need to know the students and teachers on an individual basis, know the school's curriculum, and understand how students develop and experience the world. Furthermore, librarians need to practice calm patience and help the student feel comfortable and trusting in order to optimize the questioning process. Librarians should listen more than talk and avoid jumping to conclusions. It also helps to ask the student afterward if he or she experienced success in the information task and what other RIS might be needed. Librarians should also encourage students to state what resources and strategies were most and least helpful so that the librarian can improve the art and science of questioning.

RIS INTERACTIONS IN ONLINE ENVIRONMENTS

Increasingly, students are using online Q/A services to get the information they need. Some of these services are very general, such as Yahoo Answers, or may target a very specific audience, such as a fandom site. Some libraries also provide online Q/A services, which are usually termed online/digital/virtual/24-7 reference services. Some of the most popular ones are Ask a Librarian and Credo. Two popular online reference providers are Question-Point (an OCLC platform) and Tutor.com. Most of the library online reference services originate from academic and public librarians, though multi-type consoria exist. At one point, AASL offered a similar service, but it was discontinued.

Basically, 24-7 reference service implies that the user can get help from a librarian anytime, anywhere. Technically, virual reference is "reference services initiated electronically where patrons employ computers or other technology to communicate with public services staff without being physically present" (RUSA, 2010, p. 1). In its infancy, 24-7 reference service meant leaving the librarian a telephone or e-mail message, with the expectation that the user would get an answer the next day. Nowadays, 24-7 reference service frequently exists in real time, with the user and the librarian chatting in a textual cyberspace (e.g., instant messaging model) or within a web GUI interface where both parties can look at and navigate through shared documents. For school libraries, the term "online reference service" makes the most sense, so that term will be used in this chapter.

Typical online reference service users may differ from face-to-face inquirers. They tend to be independent and self-motivated, preferring anonymity. Often they work outside the usual workday time frame, yet want convenient, just-in-time service. They are usually technologically comfortable. They have "traditional" language or physical barriers, such as need for a wheelchair or visual impairment. Some are just shy about asking for help in person. Several of these characteristics reflect typical teenager mind-sets.

For that reason alone, school librarians should consider providing online reference service because they may attract current nonusers of library services. Additionally, online reference service expands physical access to information beyond school hours and facilitates more school and community involvement. It demonstrates value-added service and thus serves as good public relations. Most importantly, though, online reference service helps students succeed. Online interaction can take many forms: embedded presence in course management systems, threaded discussions, online chats, just-in-time web conferencing, professional development webinars (Raraigh-Hopper, 2010).

As with electronic reference sources, decisions about online reference service require addressing several issues, which often impact interaction.

- Should the service be controlled in-house or outsourced? What staffing and server access are available? Usually the best solution is to join a consortium in order to share human and material resources. However, it is important that all reference librarians be trained on interacting with youth and getting to know at least Common Core State Standards and typical K–12 curriculum. Ideally, school librarians should collaborate to provide K–12-oriented online RIS.
- What kind of interface should be used? E-mail is the easiest; it is usually a good idea to have a separate e-mail address just for online service. However, e-mail is now considered for "old people and teachers" by students. Instant messaging and texting provides real-time interaction and is particularly well suited to mobile use. A CGI dialog box can facilitate e-mailing protocols and archiving but requires more technical expertise. Web conferencing that includes a "whiteboard" or other shared visual space to examine documents jointly provides the richest experience, but usually entails buying special software programs and getting training to use the product effectively, Additionally, some older computer systems might not be able to handle the interface; librarians have to consider the digital access of their school community 24-7 (e.g., "smart" phones and other mobile devices, dial-up Internet connectivity).
- What is acceptable turnaround time? In the e-mail environment, twenty-four hours is usually considered satisfactory. Even real-time chats often require further research and a follow-up contact, so the twenty-four hours applies in that situation as well. Youth can be impatient with online service, so it can be better to e-mail or text them back rather than have them wait in cyberspace while the librarian is trying off-line to find an obscure reference source. Whenever possible, the online librarian should tell the

student explicitly what process is being done while the blank screen seems to be staring them in the face.

- What kinds of queries should be handled: ready refererence, general homework, research projects? To what extent might the librarian unknowingly be doing the students' work? In that respect, having local school librarians staff online RIS helps mitigate that possibility. However, the issue begs the question: to what extent should the librarian help: giving answers, providing citations, suggesting referrals? Some questions are asked all the time, so FAQ sheets or "scripts" can be developed for those queries, serving as a way to filter questions. For regular, anticipated assignments, librarians might create pathfinders with online links to aid students. Sophisticated research projects provide a natural opportunity to teach information literacy skills and processes. Because online reference service is able to archive the "discussion," librarians can view those transcripts later on to develop guidelines for future service.

- What staffing is appropriate? Real-time interaction, in particular with sophisticated software programs, requires facility with online communication practice as well as good reference interviewing and searching skills. Again, as young people tend to equate reference service with school work, they expect that the librarian will know about school assignments.

- What kind of access should be provided? Because these services are web-based, they are broadcast publicly. A password might be appropriate to screen users. Sometimes a library card number is a means to authenticate users, though such mechanisms require further programming. Will the service be linked from the library web portal or the school web page? Should public libraries have a link to the school service? Having multiple ports of entry maximizes access, but it can also open the way for "outsiders" to monopolize the librarian's reference time.

- What funding factors need to be considered? Staffing, technical help, web design, web server hosting, Internet connectivity, and software all cost money.

- What legal and ethical issues need to be addressed: filtering, confidentiality and privacy, security, copyright, to name a few? One reason that schools are reluctant to provide access to online reference service is that the students may be guided to inappropriate websites. Furthermore, some schools have very strict filtering policies because of safety concerns. In that respect, if districts or consortia can provide a K–12 service, some of the fears can be addressed more successfully.

Online Visual Interaction

Web and video conferencing are increasingly used as part of RIS because the equipment, software, and access are becoming cheaper and easier to use.

Online conferencing provides real-time interaction and can facilitate joint use of reference resources as well as offer a means to see each other. Typically, online conferencing requires prescheduling, though low-end solutions such as voice-over-IP can be kept open passively until a request comes in.

For the past few years, librarians have been exploring RIS in virtual reality settings such as Second Life (Buckland & Dogfrey, 2010). Virtual realities, or virtual microworlds as they are sometimes termed, such as Second Life are digital constructs. All of the objects are created ultimately from algorithms performed on electronic bits of ones and zeros (off and on). Second Life provides users with digital building blocks with which to construct 3D simulated objects such as furniture, colleges, and so on. The participants in Second Life are also constructed using computer-aided design and are then situated digitally into the virtual digital landscape. Second Life is digitally stored in a server farm owned by Linden Lab. It must be noted, however, that newness does not equate to quality. Second Life exemplifies the issue of ideological connotations. It seems to have already reached the tipping point in popularity with some organizations dropping their subscriptions to this service, and advertising seeming to be more prevalent than substantial content. Furthermore, specific restrictions apply to users under eighteen years old; organizations serving youth under age sixteen have to limit user access to within the "estate." Nevertheless, the concept of virtual realities reflects the urge to imitate 3D environments.

The virtual world of Second Life and its ilk is set up to be very interactive. The user participants interact with the virtual space and with the other user participants, including librarians, in real time. Indeed, the user even interacts with his or her own avatar, which is the mechanism with which the user virtually moves about the space and communicates with others. Depending on the user's own technological skill and personality, that interaction with the avatar can be very psychically close or disengaging. The fact that the user can personalize and accessorize the avatar reflects another level of interactivity and also resonates for teens who want to explore different personalities or behaviors. As user participants customize their avatars and become more adept at moving their virtual figured representations, they can use nuanced gestures to help contextualize their communication. Second Life also permits text and voice input, which simulates face-to-face communication. In fact, video conferencing can occur in Second Life so that all digital media are available as communication tools.

Online Interactive Skills

As explained above, online reference interviewing requires additional skills beyond traditional reference interaction. RUSA has developed specific standards for online RIS. While the same respect must be observed within relationships with users, librarians need to be mindful that online communication is much more abstract since it cannot transmit visual or aural cues. Explanations need to be made more explicitly and clearly. Jargon needs to be avoided. Online users may have difficulty explaining their informational needs both because of information literacy limitations and because of language limitations. It should be noted that asynchronous questions are usually longer than synchronous ones because there is less opportunity to fine-tune the query. Machine delays and crashes can be frustrating for both parties, and even a blank screen while either person is typing or searching can be confused with logging off. As noted before, librarians must be very careful not to make assumptions about their online users, be it in terms of age, ability, knowledge, or behavior. Because students can be very sensitive and self-conscious, textual communication can be a delicate negotiation. Furthermore, in this abstract environment, school librarians need to go the extra mile to demonstrate their responsiveness to their sometimes restless students. The following tips help optimize the interview.

- Determine type of question (e.g., fact, source, research strategy) and context (school assignment, personal need, etc.).
- Use a mix of closed and open-ended questions; restate the question to make sure that it is understood by both parties. Break down complex queries into discrete steps.
- Know when to stop or contact later.
- Use a "letter correspondence" mindset.

Both face-to-face and online RIS have their advantages. Even with video conferencing, face-to-face interaction is a richer and more personalized experience. Online reference service works better when the focus is limited to digital resources. Online potentially is more convenient, at least in terms of access time, though interestingly, students are just as apt to use online reference service during school hours as after hours. One potential advantage of online reference service is transcription; if the interaction is recorded and archived, the user can review it later.

COLLABORATION

For school librarians to design and deliver information and reference services, the need for collaboration is obvious. Potential collaborators to advance information and reference services include teachers and other staff, students, parents, and other librarians. This section discusses how to establish and maintain collaborative partners and ideas for joint work.

Basics of Collaboration

The term "collaboration" appears frequently in library literature, but its meaning is sometimes misapplied. Technically, collaboration requires interdependence and a task scope substantive enough that one person would have great difficulty accomplishing that task. Both parties need to interact socially and intellectually, and they need to have a shared vision, thinking, planning, creation, and evaluation.

Different levels of interaction also exist in RIS, each reflecting significant aspects and scopes of action (Montiel-Overall, 2005).

- Networking involves informal social interaction that can lead to joint efforts. For instance, the librarian might talk with a teacher about information literacy during a staff picnic.
- Coordination reflects a formal relationship between equal partners. For instance, the classroom teacher might schedule the library's computer lab for word processing.
- Cooperation consists of a give-and-take working relationship where each party furthers its goals. For instance, a teacher might have students research social issues, and the librarian would provide a pathfinder of relevant reference sources.

It is possible for the school librarian to have different working relationships with the same party in different contexts or over time.

Partnerships

Typically, school librarians strive for partnerships, which consist of working relationships of parties with common goals and roles. Partners identify their unique competencies and resources, hoping to complement and build on them to accomplish a common purpose such as student searching skills. Successful joint planning and activities can lead to long-term sustainable partnerships.

The benefits are obvious: shared expertise, resources, planning, and assesment. However, partnerships do take time and effort, so the results need to be worth the extra work. Partnerships require sharing control, which can be uncomfortable for some. Each partner needs to learn effective modes of communication with each other, for instance; one may prefer e-mails and the other may like to text. Successful partnerships include the following elements, which were identified by Greene & Kochhar-Bryant (2003):

- leadership and vision;
- clear expectations, procedures, and policies;
- defined roles and contributions;

- individual planning and monitoring;
- adequate allocation of time, funding, and resources;
- action coordination and linking;
- action monitoring and follow-through;
- professional development;
- evaluation and follow-up of efforts.

Partnerships are dynamic, changing over time. At the start, each person needs to be knowledgeable and competent in his or her own domain and willing to share expertise and goals. It takes time to state expectations and clarify roles. With familiarity and some initial success, partners can feel freer to risk conflict in order to deal with differentes and build a mature working relationship. Otherwise, the partnership will remain at a shallow level. In addition, the context of each person changes and can impact the partnership: marital status, family demands, professional obligations, and so forth. Because of these changes, partners need to renegotiate roles and responsibilities as needed.

For partners to become and remain effective, they need to be assessed along several dimensions (Farmer, 1999):

- Assessment: Partners use a variety of strategies to assess students, resources, and services. Assessment is used to improve practice and positively impact student success.
- Planning: The librarian manager is a full partner throughout the curricular planning process, including instructional design and implementation. Information and digital literacies are integrated throughout the curriculum. All activities involving the library program are planned cooperatively. Partners modify plans in response to changing needs.
- Implementation: Partners team-teach and team-assess. Partners use and share a variety of resources and strategies.
- Commitment: Partners communicate regularly with each other and the school community. Partners coach each other naturally as needed. Partners depend on each other for support. Partnerships are long term and sustainable.

In the final analysis, the most salient question about partnership effectiveness is: "Could I have attained the same results as effectively if I had done it by myself?"

Methods of Collaboration

RIS collaborative activities abound in today's digital world. The practice of collaborative intelligence, where several people contribute to the knowledge base, expands the notion of collaboration at the creation stage.

Technology has greatly expanded the options for collaborating. Web 2.0: Cool Tools (http://cooltoolsforschools.wikispaces.com/Collaborative+Tools) has an extensive list of digital collaborative tools. Types of collaboration functions include:

- facilitated communication: e-mails, texting, instant messaging, real-time chat, threaded discussions, tracking features of word processing software;
- virtual meetings: Elluminate/Collaborate, Adobe Connect, Mikogo;
- collective information generation: wikis, Google docs, Edmodo, LibraryThing, image sharing tools (e.g., Pinterest, Flickr), collaborative "walls" (e.g., Wallwisher);
- file sharing tools: DropBox, Sendui.

As with communication in general, collaboration should acknowledge and build on each stakeholders' expertise and interests. Here are group-specific collaborative activities to consider.

With Students

- Have youth brainstorm innovative ways to incorporate technology into library RIS.
- Have youth create a library orientation video and virtual tours on mobile devices.
- Have youth help develop the library portal.
- Have teen teams review reference resources.
- Have youth do RIS publicity: displays, e-posters, podcasts, pubic service announcements, and so on.
- Have students "tag" reference resources on the library catalog.

With Classroom Teachers

- Be aware of the other's activities, ideas, and communication.
- Share each other's RIS products.
- Coordinate division of labor: planning, instruction, learning activity, assessment. Typically, the classroom teacher is responsible for content; the school librarian is responsible for resources and search strategies.
- Brainstorm together; do joint needs assessment of students' information needs and abilities.
- Work together on schoolwide initiatives and committees.

- Ask teachers to recommend reference resources.

With Administrators

- Get a clear picture of administrators' RIS expectations, and then expand on their knowledge.
- Do your homework before going to administrators.
- Volunteer to do background research for administrators.
- Develop a library RIS course for credit.
- Create a library portal as part of the school's portal.

With Parents

- Provide parent awareness and access to reference resources.
- Maintain open communication about library RIS: blogs, newsletters, and so on.
- Provide parent workshops showing how to use reference resources and supervise students' use.
- Ask parents to recommend reference resources.
- Recruit parent volunteers as reference tutors.
- Encourage parents to help fund-raise and donate to support library RIS.

With Other Librarians

- Develop a shared RIS vision.
- Communicate about research assignments and specific books: among teaching public and school librarians and bookstores.
- Arrange with public librarians to visit schools during opportune times for students to get public library cards—or include public library card application with school registration packet.
- Refer to homework assistance at the public library (librarytutor.org); promote @schoollibrary/@yourlibrary.
- Use public library bookmarks and other PR tools.
- "Like" the public library on the school library portal.
- Collaboratively produce reference tools such as pathfinders and online tutorials.
- Collaboratively design and implement reference workshops.
- Provide regional online reference services.

STUDENT ISQUADS

As students become more information savvy, they can serve as peer coaches. Just as with other types of student aide work, student iSquads can provide invaluable service to the school community. A simple model to use is apprenticeship.

As a course or co-curricular offering, students learn about reference sources and research strategies—and how to coach peers in their incorporation. Even as apprentices, students can pilot-test reference guides, making suggestions for improvements. They can also learn how to perform tasks that support RIS, such as downloading reference resoures or software programs, or creating podcasts that can focus on RIS. Apprentice iSquad students can also shadow the librarian in his or her RIS capacity and then debrief the interactions.

Once the iSquad student demonstrates competence in reference and research strategies, and can use reference sources effectively, they can concentrate on practice RIS coaching under the tutelage of a library worker. After an RIS interaction, the library worker should debrief with the student, pointing out good efforts and guiding them to more effective practices. When the iSquad student's coaching is consistently good, her or she can go "solo," even helping outside the library. iSquad students may develop specialties within RIS, such as evaluating websites, nativating database aggregators, or developing online tutorials or subject-specific depth (e.g., science, history, sports, films). Some iSquad students may like to work with peers having special needs, teach parents digital reference skills, or serve as mentors for upcoming iSquad students. iSquads can also collaborate with each other to improve RIS overall and iSquad practices in particular through face-to-face interaction and online collaborative tools.

School librarians should also address emotional and social sides of teen service: through frequent support, recognition of effort and performance, special privileges, college and job letters of recommendation, and increased authority and responsibility. At the group level, school librarians should encourage the iSquad to create a group identity through badges, mascots or avatars, taglines, or other social "mark." In addition, librarians should provide opportunities for the iSquad to socialize and celebrate benchmark accomplishments.

REFERENCES

American Association of School Librarians. (2009). *Empowering learners: Guidelines for school library programs*. Chicago: American Library Association.

Buckland, A., & Dogfrey, K. (2010). Save the time of the avatar: Canadian academic libraries using chat reference in multi-user virtual environments. *The Reference Librarian, 51*, 12–30.

Constantino, R. (Ed.). (1998). *Literacy, access, and libraries among the language minority population*. Lanham, MD: Scarecrow Press.

Dali, K. (2010). Readers' advisory in public libraries and translated fiction. *The Reference Librarian, 51*, 175–188.

Farmer, L. (2008). Predictors for success: Experiences of beginning and expert school librarians. In V. J. McClendon (Ed.), *Educational media and technology annual* (pp. 157–184). Westport, CT: Libraries Unlimited.

———. (1999). *Partnerships for lifelong learning* (2nd ed.). Worthington, OH: Linworth.

Ferrer-Vinent, I. (2010). For English, Press 1: International students' language preference at the reference desk. *The Reference Librarian, 51*, 189–201.

Greene, G., & Kochhar-Bryant, C. (2003). *Pathways to successful transition for youth with disabilities*. Upper Saddle River, NJ: Merrill Prentice Hall.

International Federation of Library Associations and UNESCO (2002). *School library guidelines*. Hague: IFLA.

Montiel-Overall, P. (2005). A theoretical understanding of TLC. *School Libraries Worldwide, 11*(2), 24–48.

Raraigh-Hopper, J. (2010). Improving library services for distance learners: A literature review. *The Reference Librarian, 51*, 69–78.

Reference and User Services Association. (2013). *Guidelines for behavioral performance of reference and information service providers*. Chicago: American Library Association. Retrieved from http://www.ala.org/rusa/resources/guidelines/guidelinesbehavioral.

——— (2010). *Guidelines for implementing and maintaining virtual reference services*. Chicago: American Library Association. Retrieved from http://www.ala.org/rusa/sites/ala.org.rusa/files/content/resources/guidelines/virtual-reference-se.pdf.

——— (2007). *Guidelines for library services to teens*. Chicago: American Library Association. Retrieved from http://www.ala.org/rusa/resources/guidelines/guidelinesteens.

———. (2003). *Professional competencies for reference and user services librarians*. Chicago: American Library Association. Retrieved from http://www.ala.org/rusa/resources/guidelines/professional.

Ross, C. (1998) Negative closure. *Reference & User Services Quarterly, 38*, 151–157.

Sarkodie-Manash, K. (Ed.). (2000). *Reference services for the adult learner*. New York: Haworth Press.

Chapter Seven

Providing Reference and Information Services Instruction

While in some libraries, instruction is an add-on, for school libraries, instruction as part of information services is a core function. The chapter begins by listing information literacy standards, then details instructional design, which offers a systematic way to approach information instruction. School librarians should determine student learning outcomes, which are often identified in content standards, Common Core State Standards, and information/digital literacy standards, all of which school librarians need to negotiate and resolve. At that point, they can then determine the curriculum that enables students to gain relevant knowledge and skills; this process needs to be done in collaboration with the entire school community. The community also has to determine the most effective structure for that curriculum: stand-alone, embedded, required, or elective. Instruction modes themselves can vary: from lecturette to constructivist; different objectives are best met with different modes of instruction and learning activities. Likewise, instruction itself might be delivered face-to-face or virtually, by the school librarian or another expert. Regardless of the instructional design or delivery, assessment of the process and the results needs to be done throughout. A sidebar discusses how to map the curriculum in terms of these different learning standards.

INFORMATION LITERACY AND LEARNING STANDARDS

Librarians have helped people locate information for centuries. Variously called library instruction, bibliographic instruction, and library user instruction, such guidance intended to help people navigate the world of recorded information. In the 1970s the phrase "information literacy" was coined to describe the skills to use a variety of information tools to solve problems (Zurkowski, 1974). Generally, information literacy has come to mean the ability to locate, evaluate, select, use, manage, and share information effectively and responsibly. The Institute of Information Literacy provides a good overview on the subject and focuses on implications for administrators and faculty (http://www.ala.org/acrl/nili/whatis.html). In recent decades, educational librarians have embraced this concept, using it as their linchpin to help students gain these competencies. Information literacy is sometimes explained as research skills (which is purposeful, task-based information literacy that might or might not be communicated). It is important to differentiate among these terms. Information literacy, unlike research skills, also includes dealing with information that one encounters or has to respond to (such as dealing with a car accident). Critical thinking addresses how to evaluate/critique a given document, but it does not include location skills, which information literacy does. Even in Common Core, which largely overlaps information literacy, the term information literacy is missing. Therefore, school librarians have to "translate" or "crosswalk" the skills and knowledge from other domains.

Several information literacy models exist, which usually focus on research process skills. The most well-known model in K–12 settings is the Big Six, which includes the following elements:

- task definition,
- information-seeking strategies,
- location of and access to information,
- use of information,
- information synthesis, and
- evaluation.

Dozens of other information literacy models exist; several are detailed at http://ictnz.com/infolitmodels.htm. Loetscher and Woolls's 2002 book *Information Literacy: A Review of the Research* remains the last major review of such models, especially in terms of K–12 practice. Notwithstanding the variations, most research process models include the stages of planning, access, comprehension, and use, with a running strand of iterative evaluation and action, which can be termed "metacognition."

Today's students have to prepare for a world that is yet to be imagined. Now more than ever, people require lifelong learning skills in order to survive constant changes. The Partnership for 21st Century Skills (2013), a consortium of public and private organiations, identified the following skills as necessary for future success:

- core subject matter: reading, writing, mathematics, twenty-first-century themes;
- life and career skills;
- learning and innovation skills: critical thinking and problem solving, communication, collaboration, and creativity;
- information, media, and technology skills.

The Common Core State Standards (CCSS), an initiative developed in 2009 by the the Council of Chief State School Officers, was a response to the federal education "Race to the Top." Its intent is to raise K–12 standards and provide a common means to measure what students need to know and do to be career and college ready by the end of twelfth grade. States have local flexibility in implementing these standards. The CCSS address English language arts and mathematics and focus on critical thinking, research, application, communication, and technology.

In determining the role that school librarians play in contributing to student performance and lifelong learning, the American Association of School Librarians (AASL) (2007) developed standards for the twenty-first-century learner, which transcend the staple "information literacy." AASL contends that the definition of information literacy has become very complex because of the expanded repertoire of resources and information tools. Thereore, AASL has as its goal for learners to use skills, resources, and tools to:

1. inquire, think critically, and gain knowledge;
2. draw conclusions, make informed decisions, apply knowledge to new situations, and create new knowledge;
3. share knowledge and participate ethically and productively as members of our democratic society;
4. pursue personal and aesthetic growth (p. 3).

Each standard includes skills, dispositions, responsibilities, and self-assessment strategies. AASL further asserts that school librarians play a vital role in helping students meet these standards because the school library program provides the most comprehensive physical and intellectual access to educational resources and offers a beneficial learning environment for engaging in productve information experiences. Many of the CCSS processes mirror information literacy and AASL learning standards. In fact, AASL developed a crosswalk document that aligns its learning standards with CCSS: http://www.ala.org/aasl/standards-guidelines/crosswalk.

INSTRUCTION TO IMPROVE INFORMATION BEHAVIORS

While it's true that some young people learn without formal instruction, most skills, including information literacy and other twenty-first-century learning skills, require explicit instruction. General learning skills can be hard to pin down. Information literacy is a fairly recent term relative to other academic domains and is often omitted in school curriculum. Furthermore, who is qualified to teach information literacy? Certainly, school librarians have the knowledge, and most states require school librarians to also have a teaching credential. School librarians can collaborate with subject teachers to conduct instruction that addresses information behaviors. Information literacy and competent information behavior, like reading, are the entire school community's responsibility; that said, the school librarian can serve as coordinator.

In the role of teacher, the school librarian helps the school community learn how to physically and intellectually access the information they need. Typically, instruction is short, such as how to use a dictionary. It may be geared toward a group, with one-to-one follow-up differentiated instruction. Alternatively, instruction may occur on a just-in-time basis for one person, such as using an endnote feature in a word processing program. Librarians also use a train-the-trainer model with small groups of students or teachers who then train their peers. The underlying pattern tends to be dynamic and responsive, instructing based on expressed need, rather than proactive or arbitrarily scheduled by preset curriculum units.

Regardless of the model used, or aspect of information literacy addressed, the most powerful instruction and learning occurs in authentic information tasks developed collaboratively by the subject teacher and librarian. Each partner brings unique expertise to the table; together they model the kind of cooperative learning that students should undertake themselves as lifelong learners. For instance, when a class is studying the impact of the Dust Bowl, the school librarian can show students how to locate relevant images from the Library of Congress's American Memory digital collections.

MAPPING THE CURRICULUM

While it makes sense to develop a library scope and sequence information literacy/learning curriculum, approaching it as a schoolwide initiative is more effective. Otherwise, such a curriculum will be considered solely the responsibility of the school librarian, with no acknowledgment that anyone else has to care. One effective approach is to map the school's curriculum in light of AASL learning standards. The entire faculty can identify those lessons, learning activities, and assignments that address or presuppose information literacy/learning student learning outcomes. Content teachers should also indicate whether they teach the skill or have the librarian do so. Underlying conditions for information literacy also need to be addressed, such as citation style guides or research project rubrics. By identifying course efforts, the librarian can determine gaps in concepts and skills and then negotiate with teachers to make sure that the remaining standards can be systematically taught (Farmer, 2002).

INSTRUCTIONAL DESIGN

Curriculum and its development can occur on several levels: from an international curriculum, such as media literacy, to a single-incident training about one skill. As mentioned above, much library instruction exists as just-in-time, informal training: targeted help to solve an immediate information task problem. Such short-term guidance should not be dismissed, and it is certainly appreciated by the requester. Nevertheless, school librarians should also design instruction systematically to ensure that every student has predictable opportunities to learn and practice efficient information behavior.

Fundamentally, formal education tries to identify what learners need to know and do over time to be successful and productive members of society, based on social norms and expectations. The curriculum identifies the content matter that learners should know and be able to apply. Content standards describe the the level of competence expected of the student. In this light, information literacy and AASL's learning standards may be considered curricular content. Some states have an explicit, separate set of information behavior (i.e., information literacy/learning) standards, such as California, while other states, such as Florida, choose to embed these kinds of standards into existing content standards. In any case, these standards should be a schoolwide endeavor that transcends any one set of courses. Policies, hiring and teacher support, allocation of resources, and normative behavior and expectations all play a role in curriculum design and implementation. Curriculum development should also consider social forces and cultural sensitivity.

Information behavior instructional goals and objectives emerge from the content and standards. Goals can be more general, such as "comply with copyright law," but objectives need to be SMART: specific, measurable, achievable, relevant, and time bound. For instance, one objective for a five-minute quiz might be: "The student correctly identifies copyright and publication dates in print resources." All goals and objectives needs to be developmentally appropriate: in terms of information needs and typical youth behaviors, as well as cognitive, physical, and psychological degrees of maturity.

At the same time that the objectives are developed, the assessment method should also be determined so that efforts will be aligned. Quizzes may be used to measure recall, and writing can capture thinking patterns and conceptual knowledge, but problem solving and other applications of knowledge

Table 7.1. Research Presentation Rubric

	Introductory 0–1	Acceptable 2–3	Proficient 4–5	Score
Assessing Resources				
Variety of reference materials	Student evaluates three print and five nonprint resources from the same or similar sources (such as articles from the same journal).	Student evaluates three print and five nonprint resources, each from unique sources.	Student evaluates more than three print and five nonprint resources from varied sources with a rationale for the selection of the resource.	
Evaluating Credibility of Resources				
Evaluating each resource for topic-specific usefulness in a research setting	Many of the resources are not specifically related to the topic. Further research on appropriate resources is necessary.	All of the resources are directly related to the topic.	All of the resources directly relate to the topic. Some of the resources provide unique points of view that will enrich the discussion of the topic in unanticipated ways.	
Evaluating each resource for reliability	Many of the resources selected offer little or no indication of reliability such as authorship, accuracy, and/or currency of information.	Most of the resources selected demonstrate reliability of information such as authorship, accuracy, and currency.	All of the resources selected demonstrate reliability through authorship, accuracy, and currency of information.	
Use of rubric	Use of the rubric does not indicate understanding of the criteria or the resource.	Use of the rubric indicates some understanding of the criteria or the resource.	Use of the rubric indicates understanding of the criteria and appropriate evaluation of the resource.	

Presenting conclusions from research	Conclusions are presented based on the evaluation of the resources. The conclusions cannot be generalized and do not extend experience into teaching.	Generalizations are made from the experience of evaluating the resources that inform further searches on the topic.	Generalizations are made based on the experience that inform further searches on this topic and other topics. Guideline statements are suggested for evaluating resources with students.
Oral Presentation			
Effectiveness of presentation	Presentation did not engage class, lacked continuity, was disorganized.	Presentation caught the attention of the class; content was conveyed.	Presentation sustained the attention of the class in an informative and entertaining way, leaving the audience with a strong understanding of the generalizations and conclusions of the research.

Total Score

Skill Level:
Introductory 19 points or less; Acceptable 14–21 points; Proficient 22–30 points

usually require authentic tasks to assess the various factors that lead to competency. Most schools use rubrics to identify and operationalize each performance criterion, as well as indicate levels of competence.

Even if information behavior is not explicitly identified in school curriculum, school librarians can still collaborate with subject teachers to design instruction that involves the school library program. While it is most effective to start from the point of curriculum development itself, entering the design process at any stage is helpful. Even just providing a cart of relevant print materials for a class assignment enables students to choose information resources that can match their interests and reading levels, which one textbook cannot hope to achieve for all students in the class.

Resources

Needs assessment should drive curriculum, which in turn drives instructional design. Standardized texts seldom provide the contextualized information required for optimum learning, so choosing relevant and appropriate resources is a critical instructional design decision. Fortunately, providing resources in support of curriculum is the most basic function done by librarians. Instructional design, especially as it incorporates technology, offers a great opportunity for librarians to expand this role.

Careful selection of resources is particularly important since the decision needs to consider the curricular content, the nature of the users, the ways that the resources are used, the form of instruction, and the learning environment overall. These factors impact the evaluation of the potential resource in terms of format, images and sound, language, learning preferences, ease of use, availability, and cost. Digital resource choice also has to consider physical access issues, especially in terms of the still remaining digital divide. Resources may be clustered into the following categories, depending on their use:

- content-centric: subject-specific information, from textbooks to civil rights videos;
- production-centric: resources that facilitate content manipulation and presentation, such as hardware and productivity "suites";
- task-specific: resources used for a specific information process, such as a concept map for brainstorming prior knowledge about a topic.

School librarians need to consider the learning objective and its context as they independently or collaboratively select those materials. Furthermore, as technology is incorporated into education, instructors need to differentiate between learning *about* technology (content-centric approach) and learning *with* technology (production-centric). Further complicating the issue, digital resources, which would be considered content-centric, need production-centric equipment in order to be accessed. It should be also noted that the core element is the information within the resource; perhaps just one encyclopedia entry or one video clip is needed.

A specific type of resource that is increasingly popular is a "learning object," which is a self-contained digital resource, such as a simulation, presentation, or assessment. The learning object can be repurposed for several courses. The website http://www.merlot.org exemplifies a repository of learning objects. Such repositories, or databases, would be a natural fit for librarians to develop. The curation chapter explains learning objects in more depth.

Sometimes existing resources need to be modified in order to align with the instructional design. To a large extent, adaptations fall under "fair use" copyright law, even in online instruction (thanks to the TEACH Act); nevertheless, librarians should be sure that they and the rest of the school community comply with copyright law, which can be particularly problematic when course materials are available publicly online. The chapter on curation details issues in packaging preexisting information.

Instructional Delivery

This part of instructional design—the delivery—is what most subject teachers and librarians focus on. The learning experience can occur anywhere, and several decisions lead up to that delivery: space, grouping, staffing, timing, teaching interaction, student activity. The human element is key in delivery: who will do the actual instruction? Librarians often collaborate, but the teaching role has to be negotiated carefully. How will instructional delivery change in response to student behaviors? Even at the delivery point, instructional design is evaluated and modified as needed.

Time Issues

The school librarian and collaborating teacher need to negotiate the time frame of the instruction. Will it be a onetime lesson, a unit, or an entire course? How long will one session last? How much time will pass between instructional sessions? If information behavior instruction is embedded into an existing course, how will the instructional time be split?

Another timing issue involves the sequencing of the content matter. Content and its application build on prior experience. What prerequisite knowledge and skills are needed? When integrating content and information behavior, how does the sequencing of one set of objectives impact the other? In some cases, content may be organized in modular form such that the order is not significant within the total unit as long as the ultimate objectives are met.

Space Issues

Where will instruction occur? The obvious choices are the classroom and the library, but other sites might be considered: computer lab, multipurpose room, hallway, outdoors, off-campus, online. The choice might depend on who is instructing, what resources are needed, what kind of task is involved, or simple convenience. With web conferencing, the librarian might stay in the library, teaching virtually with the students interacting in the classroom.

It should be noted that online delivery requires special attention because it typically offers fewer sensory and social experiences. Instructional design has to compensate by explicitly building opportunities for social interaction and providing more opportunities to communicate in alternative ways. Some instructors state that online delivery actually leads to more participation and more thoughtful reflection because students have more time and chances to share inner thoughts. Hybrid education seems to be the most effective mode because it enables instructors to focus on student interaction and guided practice in class and gives students autonomy to gain knowledge according to their own needs and preferences on their own time.

Staffing

Who will instruct? It is important for the school librarian and subject teacher to share their content and instructional expertise. There are many ways to share this responsibility: by content matter, by task, by part of the lesson and learning activity, by location, by instructional method, or by shared interactive dialogue. As partners work with each other and get to know each other's preference and then make adjustments as appropriate.

Particularly in elementary school settings, the librarian is likely to work with an entire class, instructing a variety of individuals, several of whom may have different special needs. The teacher should accompany the class, not only in order to make sure that the content is relevant and the learning activity is clear, but also because the teacher works with these children daily and knows how to address their special needs effectively. The librarian does have the advantage of interacting with the students every year and witnessing their development, but specific group dynamics impact how children behave. Ideally, the librarian and teacher should develop the learning activity together so that accommodations can be considered ahead of time, thereby optimizing each child's learning experience in the library. Typically, the librarian demonstrates the basic concept and process to be learned and gets the class started working. The librarian then can work with a smaller group who need more scaffolding, such as English language learners. The teacher might work with another group such as children with Asperger's syndrome. The classroom teacher and librarian thus complement each other.

Instructional Methods

Instruction may include a variety of strategies even within one lesson. Instructors should have a broad repertoire of instructional strategies that they can draw upon when students fail to succeed somewhere along the way. Typically, factual information, such as using the library catalog, is most efficiently learned through direct instruction while more complex concepts and problem solving, such as intellectual property conflicts, are handled better through constructivist methods. For procedural knowledge and motor skills, demonstration and hands-on learning works best. Attitudinal learning requires emotional engagement; active role-play enables students to model the desired behavior. Instructional methods also reveal control issues: direct instruction is teacher-controlled while group work is more student-controlled.

One unique feature of information behavior instruction is the use of inquiry and questions as means to guide learners in ways to locate and use reference materials. This approach links reference service (how to find information for users), where the user acts as a consumer, with reference instruction, where users learns how to help others find information for themselves. School librarians also have to keep in mind that students have different learning preferences, and some students may need scaffolding.

Student Participation

Just as instructional methods vary, so too do learning methods vary. The main driver in determining the nature of student participation is the intended objective. However, in most cases, there are several ways to meet that standard, and students should develop a repertoire of ways to learn. Some of the factors to consider include:

- mind styles: abstract versus concrete, sequential versus random;
- psychology: field dependent (contextual) versus field independent;
- timing: reflective versus impulsive action;
- multiple intelligences: linguistic, spatial, musical, kinesthetic, logical, social, intrapersonal, naturalist, spiritual;
- social: independent versus collaborative;
- environment: culture, experience, educational structure, situation.

Student groupings can enable students to learn from each other and complement their skills. For example, pair-shares help students exchange perspectives. Triads help students pool ideas and develop leadership skills. Teams of four to six enable students to create complex projects such as videos and generate collective intelligence on rich topics such as a social issue. Even in group learning, students need to be personally accountable and demonstrate individual competency individually; in the video example, one student might be in charge of scripting and another student would do the camera work.

In the final analysis, school librarians should create a positive and comfortable learning environment and structure learning for meaning. School librarians should link objectives and content to students' interests, engaging them both cognitively and emotionally. School librarians also need to incorporate social aspects of learning. They should provide a variety of relevant resources from which students can choose and enable students to demonstrate competence in several ways. School librarians need to give students time to process and evaluate their own learning. They also need to provide specific and timely feedback, which can also help students adjust their own learning. As much as possible, school librarians should encourage students to be not only consumers of information but also producers of information, expressing themselves creatively.

LEARNING ACTIVITY COLLABORATIVE PLANNING CHECKLIST

Information from Farmer, 2009, p. 72. With permission from Libraries Unlimited.

- What are the desired student outcomes in terms of knowledge, skills, and attitudes? What evidence will indicate their ability? How will they be assessed?
- What content and information literacy standards are being addressed? In terms of information literacy, do students need to locate and evaluate information, or do they need to focus on extracting information from preselected sources?
- What prerequisite knowledge and skills do they need to accomplish the desired outcome? Who will diagnose those prerequisites? How will students gain that knowledge?
- What resources are needed? How do they address content and student needs?
- What resources are available in the library or accessed from the library? If resources need to be gathered from another location, what conditions and deadlines must be met?
- What resources, including teaching and learning aids, need to be created or modified? Under what conditions and time lines must they be made?
- What instruction is needed? Is introduction, review, or extension needed? Who will provide it—and under what conditions?

- What learning tasks will students be doing? What activities will they practice in order to accomplish their assignment independently? Who will check for understanding and provide feedback?
- What information and directions (for example, handouts) will be given to students? Who will produce and disseminate them?
- Where will teaching and learning occur? What arrangements need to be made in order to ensure the appropriate learning environment?
- What is the time frame for the teaching and learning? Do students need extra time to learn prerequisite skills, such as scanning images? Will some students need more time in the library than others; if so, how will they be supervised?
- How will students be grouped for learning: the whole class, small collaborative groups, or individual efforts?
- How will differentiation be addressed? What resources and instruction need to be added or modified to accommodate diverse populations (for example, different learning styles, gender differences, English language learners, students with special needs, and the gifted and talented)? What physical changes need to be made? What interpersonal factors need to be addressed?
- How will teaching and learning be assessed? Who will do it? When? How will that information be used to inform future teaching and learning?

DEALING WITH MAJOR RESEARCH PROJECTS

When helping students do major research projects, librarians need to think about ways to frame the task, provide guidance in research location strategies, encourage deep researching, and contextualize it. Usually for a big research project, students should consider these steps:

1. Get background information by consulting encyclopedias and textbooks. Pay attention to major headings and key terms. Clarify definitions.
2. Clarify the information task. Identify prior knowledge and what information needs to be gained.
3. Develop a first "run" research strategy. Identify possible types of information sources. Identify places and people where collections of relevant information are likely to be found. Based on the available time, determine how wide an information net to cast; for instance, is interlibrary loan a realistic idea?
4. Document steps: keywords, access tools, sources, links.

5. Use access tools, such as bibliographies, indexes, directories, and database aggregators.
6. Find facts in specialized reference resources.
7. Find current facts in periodicals and other mass media.
8. Try alternative sources such as interviewing.
9. Alternate between general and specific (broad and narrow) resources.
10. Review citations listed in resources as a possible redirection of efforts.
11. Review resources and research strategy in light of the information task. Consider revising tactics or redirecting the task.
12. Make research deep. Unearth it: get at the issues. Question it: test, challenge, and critique information. Analyze it: examine, dissect, refine information. Prove it: argue, support, verify, justify your stance. Generalize it: contextualize and compare information.
13. Make research broad. Connect it: link information with likely and unlikely ideas and experiences. Picture it: concretize, model, and represent information in different ways. Extend it: what are its implications, consider "what if?"
14. Take care of loose ends. Does the final product satisfy the information task? Conduct a targeted research strategy to fill in remaining gaps or questions. That's why it's called RE-search.
15. Read aloud or share the final product to make sure it accurately communicates your message.

Elementary students tend to be novice information users. As student populations progress through school, they reflect an ever increasing variety of experiences and competencies. Instructional strategies should match the research skills of the user, helping them advance from one stage to another. He and Jacobson (1996) explained how to differentiate research instruction, depending on the users' information behavior sophistication. For example, beginning researchers have little research or technology experience, limited reading skills, and unsophisticated critical thinking. Because they need much support, such students should be given a few preselected sources that are structured for easy retrieval of information. School librarians should provide simple searching models and should monitor such students closely. In contrast, intermediate researchers tend to start off well but may get frustrated if their customary strategies and resources do not satisfy the information task. They may also have difficulty evaluating sources. School librarians should suggest simple and complex resources in various formats and encourage these users to refocus and persevere. Advanced researchers tend to be lifelong learners and avid readers, who communicate well and are well organized. School librarians should show them sophisticated research strategies and challenge their thinking.

SAMPLE SOCIAL JUSTICE LEARNING ACTIVITY

Lesson Title: Adapting (to) the Environment

Grade Level:3

Subject: Science

Lesson Overview: Lately, students have witnessed how natural and human disasters such as Hurricane Katrina and the Gulf of Mexico oil spill impact living organisms (including humans). This activity shows how longer-term environmental changes impact wildlife. New Zealand is an interesting locale to explore because it enables students to see another part of the world and tie environmental issues globally.

Time Frame: one class period; second class period for cyberactivism activity
Learning Objectives: Learners will:

- Identify New Zealand plants and animals and their environments.
- Identify changes in their environment and how those changes impacted New Zealand plants and animals.
- Identify ways to improve the environment.

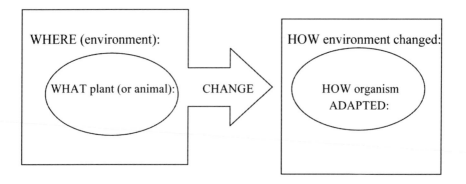

Figure 7.1. Organism adaption.

Science Standards (Aligned with Common Core)

- Students know living things cause changes in the environment in which they live: some of these changes are detrimental to the organism or other organisms, and some are beneficial.
- Students know when the environment changes, some plants and animals survive and reproduce; others die or move to new locations.

Library Standards (Aligned with Common Core)

- Identify a problem that needs information by asking how, what, where, when, or why questions.
- Use specialized content-area print and digital resources to locate information.
- Apply techniques for organizing notes in a logical order (e.g., outlining, webbing, thinking maps, and other graphic organizers).
- Select information appropriate to the problem or question at hand.
- Determine if the information answers a simple question.
- Select appropriate information technology tools and resources to interact with others for a specific purpose.

Resources

- technology: Internet-connected demonstration computer with data projector and screen; at least one computer for every two students
- http://www.kcc.org.nz/wildlife-and-wild-places
- writing tools and surfaces
- supplies for vocabulary building
- worksheet graphic organizer for each student (see figure 7.1)

Planning for Diverse Learners

- Have students work in pairs (one typical and one with needs, such as language or physical limitations).
- Have students share equipment if there is limited access to it.
- Pair English learners with native English speakers.
- Pair typical and differently abled students.
- Provide choice of information sources.
- Provide more structure for the task or divide the steps into substeps.
- Allow students to express their thoughts through art.

Instructional Strategies and Learning Activities

1. Prepare for the lesson by previewing website. Set up equipment. Print graphic organizer. Create vocabulary cards for word wall/chart as appropriate (e.g., organism, habitat, adaptation, biome, environment).

2. Ask students what environmental changes might impact plants. Ask them how plants respond/adapt (or not). Prompts can include: plant moved inside (plants bend toward light), rain (plants blossom), or frost or drought (die). Ask the same question about animals. Ask what the basis is for environment change (answers: weather, natural disasters, humans). Remind students of Katrina and the Gulf of Mexico oil spill.

3. Divide the class into pairs, and have each group choose one plant or animal found at http://www.kcc.org.nz/ wildlife-and-wild-places.

4. Have groups log onto the website and identify the organism, environment, environmental change, and adaptation using the graphic organizer. Then have similar groups (plants, birds, mammals, etc.) compare findings.

5. As a class, process and synthesize the findings in terms of environment, changes, adaptations. Compare plants and animals.

6. Ask students if such changes and adaptations occur locally; solicit concrete examples. Ask how local organisms, environments, and adaptations differ or resemble those of New Zealand.

7. Ask how humans can improve the environment to positively impact organisms. Become a cyberactivist: http://www.kcc.org.nz/become-cyber-activist. Ask students how New Zealanders have responded to the issue. Have students brainstorm ways that they can help local organisms adapt or keep healthy. Ask students to explore this site and think of ways that they can take action.

Variations

- Focus just on animals.
- Focus on one biome.
- Study a local habitat: http://courses.bio.indiana.edu/L222-Reynolds/student/s-l_02/Bin1/Bin1.htm.
- Take photographs or locate pictures of plants that have adapted.

Student Assessment: Learners are assessed via observation of class participation and online behavior and their graphic organizers. Criteria for assessment include:

- accurate and complete description of organism, environment, change, and adaptation;
- accurate and insightful description of environmental impact (negative and positive) on organisms;
- appropriate use of graphic organizer.

REFERENCES

American Association of School Librarians. (2007). *Standards for the 21st-century learner*. Chicago: American Library Association.

Farmer, L. (2002). Building information literacy through a whole school reform approach. *Knowledge Quest, 29*(3), 20–24.

———. (2009). *Your school library: Check it out!* Westport, CT: Libraries Unlimited.

He, P., & Jacobson, T. (1996). What are they doing with the Internet? *Internet Reference Services Quarterly, 1*(1), 31–51.

Loetscher, D., & Woolls, B. (2002). *Information literacy: A review of the research* (2nd ed.). San Jose, CA: Hi Willow.

Partnership for 21st Century Skills. (2013). *Framework for 21st century learning*. Washington, DC: Partnership for 21st Century Skills. Retrieved from http://www.p21.org/overview/skills-framework.

Zurkowski, P. (1974). *The information service environment: Environment relationships and priorities*. Washington, DC: National Commission on Libraries and Information Science.

Chapter Eight

Curating Reference and Information Services

Curation, selecting and organizing information, has become a popular value-added information function. School librarians have curated and packaged information for years: bibliographies, pathfinders, webliographies, themed bookmarks and displays. This chapter discusses the process of curating and designing information packages, addressing content and format issues. Another "old" related service is selective dissemination of information, which has been updated with RSS (Really Simple Syndication) feeds and individualized information spaces. Web 2.0 tools further expand the concept of curating to facilitate group-generated curation, be it by librarians or students. In fact, school librarians increasingly add curation as a "cool" way for students to gain information literacy and "own" their own research. A sidebar discusses how school librarians can take curation into the public relations arena.

WHAT IS CURATION?

The word "curation" originally meant to have a cure or charge. Today's curator is a person who has a charge as a manager or steward. According to the International Council of Museums (2001), the curator is the content specialist who is responsible for the collection, from deciding which items to collect and documenting the acquisition process and registration (similar to cataloging), to displaying, loaning, and maintaining its physical condition. The curator maintains a record of the item's provenance: the creator and the people who owned and maintained the item before the museum acquired it. The curator also researches the item's context and significance and the creator's influence. The curator shares that research with peers and the public through publications and exhibits. Curators interpret selected items and develop supporting documentation and workshops for those exhibits, along with being in charge of displaying the chosen items (including their sequencing and layout). Sometimes an artist curates one exhibit, doing the background research and organization, although the permanent curator or registrar gathers the items, verifies their authenticiy, and develops searchable repositories for them. They relate the digital collection through ontologies, done using metadata and the semantic web (Watry, 2007).

Usually the term "curation" is misapplied to library reference and information service since provenance is usually not an issue. Neither do librarians usually conduct in-depth background research when they display items in the library. Most school libraries do not spend a great effort on preservation with an eye to long-term stewardship. Instead, librarians focus on ways to optimize the collection's use. The act of selecting resources and researching their significance is a typical research project for students. Similar to traditional curation, research-based projects can include interpretation, organization, and communication. Thus, rather than giving much context to resources, school librarians tend to teach students how to conduct such curation-type of research. For instance, middle school students might create a virtual expedition of Lewis and Clark using Google Maps and inserting quotes from their journals and images that represent what they found. The students would cite the source of each artifact included and describe its significance.

PACKAGING INFORMATION

The school community often needs help locating and using reference sources. While personal interaction constitutes an effective means of instruction, other methods can complement that approach. Those aids and resources offer assistance when staff are occupied with others and address the learning differences of users. The term "packaged information" refers to transformation and recombination of information, such as extracts and citations for different uses or audiences. Packaged information comes in several formats and may serve a variety of functions, including public relations. Some examples of packaged information include bibliographies, study guides, tutorials, photo albums, posters, podcasts, and orientation videos. Digital formats facilitate repurposing the same information, morphing an outline into a Power-Point presentation or hyperlinked web page, as needed. As long as the information sources are credited ("anchoring" it) and intellectual property rights are observed, school librarians are seeing advantages of combining and synthesizing information in different content "containers" as a value-added service for their users.

As school librarians plan how to package information as a product, they need to consider the following factors:

- What is the objective? Informational, instructive, promotional, recreational? Is the audience supposed to build conceptual (i.e., ideas), procedural (i.e., how-to skills), or declarative knowledge (i.e., facts)? The objective should meet some kind of user need.
- Who is the audience? What age and group of students? Which teachers? Which support staff? Which administrators? Which parents? Which community members? Whenever possible, the product should demonstrate responsiveness to a specific target audience because each group has unique motives and needs.
- What is the message? There are many possibilties: Here are the answers. The library is here to help. Here's how you can do it. The message may be general or very specific.
- How will the product be disseminated? Through the library portal? Via a school publication? At a face-to-face event? In the school's hallways? As a phone message? As a Tweet?
- What are the resources needed—and what is available? Human, material, financial, time?
- What is the format? Varieties of print? Audio? Visual? Multimedia? Digital?
- What is the tone? Casual? Scholarly? Calm or excited? Formal or informal?
- What is the language? English? Non-English? Simplified English?

School librarians should pilot-test any product to make sure it is readable and engaging for the target audience. In any case, the message should be clear and consistent. It is also a good idea to assess the effectiveness of the product. For instance, if the objective is to promote reading, then the librarian should see more people reading, maybe checking out reading materials, and hopefully performing better in class and on reading tests.

PURPOSE-SPECIFIC INFORMATION PACKAGING

The most common type of information packaging is organizational: selecting and organizing resources based on the user's needs. Be it a reserve shelf or cart, a bibliography or webliography of sources, a database or repository, or a course "reader," these "packages" help people access the information they need. Typically, the school librarian collaborates with subject matter experts, be they classroom teachers or support specialists such as nurses, to identify the type of materials wanted to satisfy the information need. School librarians might well consult other information professionals or existing compendia of sources, such as the LibGuide community or an existing bibliography, to choose appropriate sources. The resulting project may serve a onetime lesson purpose or provide a canon for a department. Those mini-collections should be tagged or otherwise indexed to help users find the specific information needed.

Information packaging may involve extracting information from various resources and synthesizing them into a coherent product such as a literature review or position paper. The most obvious product would be background research for an educational issue such as year-round scheduling or strategies to help English language learners. Another excellent example of information synthesis is guidelines, such as copyright practice.

At an even deeper level, school librarians might interpret information from various sources. Extending the idea of copyright, developing guidelines for determining fair use of materials requires careful analysis and interpretation (and librarians should place a note on such guidelines that they are not legal experts—unless they have the legal credentials to prove so). Normally, interpretation requires in-depth specialized information and probably some element of values, but where that exists, such as expertise in special education, the librarian should feel confident in sharing that knowledge.

Information packaging can also be categorized in terms of its focus. For instance, library-centric information packages would share information about library resources and services. Information literacy-related packages would help users interact with informtion more effectively. FAQs can also serve as a library-centric service to explain how to use databses or cite resources. User-centric information packages fulfill a need expressed by the user, such as a classroom teacher or group (e.g., international students). RSS feeds can provide users automatic notices about topics that they have identified.

GETTING CURRENT ABOUT RESEARCH

A library-led needs assessment found that students needed to improve their research skills. The school librarian needed to make sure those research skills were identified and consistently presented across curricula. At a faculty meeting, these gaps were discussed, and possible interventions were brainstormed. Among the problems was the existence of an outdated and little-used school research handbook. While the English department was approached to update the old guide, it was decided that the school librarian should spearhead this effort. The school librarian aligned the research steps to the school's new list of required research skills and to the AASL standards. A committee of academic department representatives and the school librarian reviewed and modified the handbook. Sample students also gave valuable feedback, including thoughts about wording, which was incorporated into the final product. A supplemental teacher's guide was also created to help faculty instruct students in research processes. The committee made sure that the handbook could be used as a "consumable" workbook and that students and teachers could take one page/step of it as a research process focus worksheet. Committee members pilot-tested the research handbook with their classes and polished the handbook. The final version of the research handbook was given to all faculty and students and was posted on the library's web page for easy access at school and home. To measure the impact of the research handbook, the same assessment methods were used at the end of the semester as were used one year prior for the baseline needs assessment. Among the findings were the following:

- Great use was made of the research guides by students and teachers.
- More attention was made to research process along with research product.
- More students completed research assignments, and work was more solid.
- Resources were cited more often and more accurately.
- Less plagiarism was evident.
- The school librarian was more involved in the research process, including the assessment of research products.

FORMAT-SPECIFIC INFORMATION PACKAGING

As school librarians and other school community members curate information, they need to choose the most effective format to convey the content. With technology, the options have increased, as this list reflects. In addition, the same content can be repurposed into different formats to meet the information needs of different audiences or contexts.

- poster: for attention-getting, graphical synthesis; promotes visual literacy;
- collage: to use existing sources in visually and contextually dramatic way;
- graph: to display data analysis;
- bulletin board: to display variety of information attractively; promotes visual literacy;
- display/exhibit: to display variety of information, including 3D; promotes visual literacy;

- online image sharing applications: to broadcast visual information; good for collaborative efforts;
- play/skit: for kinesthetic, interactive examination of issues holistically;
- game: to engage participants in interactive learning;
- slide show: to show visual elements in meaningful sequence;
- video: for permanent documentation of information processes and library orientations;
- spreadsheet: to display statistical data in chart form;
- authoring tool: for interactive presentation that combines formats;
- web page: for wide-audience presentation that combines formats;
- tutorials: for self-paced learning activities.

Here are some details on creating other effective products:

Pathfinders help users locate thematic reference and other information resources. They are usually structured as follows: topical information, relevant key terms, principal reference sources, relevant classification numbers.

Brochures are a common handout at library orientation and can also be used for relaying specific information, such as intellectual property, in a compact and attractive way. Two-sided tri-fold brochures are the most common format. The cover is on the right third of side one and details are presented in short sections (often bulleted) on side two. The left-hand third of side one summarizes the key points, and the center of side one is reserved for library contact information. Graphics should complement the text.

Databases and repositories provide a searchable collection of information sources. Fields and their names should reflect user queries; pull-down menus can optimize search results.

Blogs typically address different aspects of a broad topic such as reading promotion or information services. They tend to be somewhat informal and need to add posts frequently. Embedded links and media make the blog more attractive. Comments make blogs more engaging, but the librarian needs to monitor them for appropriateness and relevance.

Podcasts are web-based audio files (video pocasts are called vidcasts). They can provide information, such as booktalks or fun facts, and they can instruct. Podcasts need to be scripted tightly but shouldn't sound as if they are being read. Introductory and end theme music help provide consistent branding (see http://wiki.creativecommons.org/Content_Directories for an extensive list of Creative Commons audio sources). Most podcasts are less than five minutes long; some of the most effective ones are less than a minute long, serving as informational advertisements. Podcasts usually start with a strong engaging or startling message, develop the idea—including benefits for the listener—and finish with library contact information.

Learning objects are self-contained, modular learning aids such as simulations, presentations, and assessments. They may be repurposed for use in different contexts and are usually in digital format to facilitate their access and use. Learning objects work very well for librarians who can incorporate them into several instructional arenas. Learning objects need to have high-quality content, be easy to use independently, and reflect good instructional design. MERLOT, a well-known repository of learning objects, peer reviews each potential learning object using the criteria described at http://taste. merlot.org/evaluationcriteria.html/.

Library portals serve as online information gateways, as discussed in the access chapter. They facilitate physical and intellectual access to resources as well as offer a means to interact with the library. Much curation-related thinking goes behind the development: identifying the objectives, selecting the content, formatting it, maintaining it, and incorporating interactive aspects into the website. Valenza (2007) identified the following elements of outstanding school library websites: OPAC presence and links to other libraries' OPACS, aggregator database access, e-books, news, pathfinders, web search tools, online reference resources, homework help, college and career planning sources, and online reference service links.

DYNAMIC PACKAGING OF INFORMATION

Especially with the advent of social media, packaging information has gained a dynamic presence. Information sources can be curated as part of the creation and dissemination process, and curation can be accomplished collectively. School librarians should leverage social media to provide relevant curated information.

With the increase in access to digital information, the concept of personal learning spaces has gained credence. As information users construct an information need profile, they can be alerted to new relevant digital resources automatically. RSS feeds enable the user to subscribe to an information provider, who matches new resources with the user's profile as determined by metadata and then "pushes" the document to the user, usually through an RSS reader or even e-mail. In this case, the RSS feature becomes the packaging vehicle. Feedly, Digg, Newsvide, Curata, and Pulse each have unique features to recommend them. In this model, the librarian establishes the infrastructure for users to create profiles and receive relevant information; careful tagging of metadata can make or break this information service.

Another trend is group curation, where people with similar interests and expertise collaboratively build a body of knowledge. A good case could be made that Wikipedia exemplifies this collective intelligence as people contribute articles that synthesize a specific topic through careful selection of information sources. Wikis are the de facto standard forum for such group curation. Typically, groups of experts form, often based on professional networking and peer review. They identify a topic to curate and establish criteria for selection and description of information resources. Sometimes each person in the group takes the lead in a specific facet of the topic to delegate responsibility and expertise; again, Wikipedia is a stellar example of this model. Few librarian groups take advantage of group curation. Theoretically, a school district of librarians could create a collection of reference websites, with each librarian taking responsibility for one subject matter at one developmental level (i.e., elementary, middle school, high school). The result could be a robust searchable collection or repository of digital reference sources that would not unduly burden any one librarian but would rather leverage each person's expertise and scale up librarians' educational contributions.

School librarians should encourage students to practice curation functions such as selection, annotation, intepretation, synthesis, organization, and presentation. Group curation offers a way to generate substantial packages of information in various forms. The product can be as simple as a wiki, Pinterest board, or Delicious stack. The key is developing criteria for selection and incorporation.

BRANDING

Branding distinguishes a line of products and builds connotations that lead to valuing and loyalty. Nike, National Public Radio, and Girl Scouts exemplify this approach. The American Library Association has a @yourlibrary campaign: to create memorable branding and help libraries around the world by providing an easily recognizable brand that libraries can adopt and leverage at the local level. All of the communication has a consistent look and tone that reinforces the instructional design. In general, posters and flyers should have one message and one graphic; supporting documents can have more detail. InfoPeople (http://infopeople.org) is a good example of effective instructional design branding. As school librarians curate information, they should brand it in order to build their credibility and profile in the school community.

REFERENCES

International Council of Museums. (2001). *Statutes of the International Council of Museums.* Paris, France: International Council of Museums.

Valenza, J. K. (2007). Discovering a descriptive taxonomy of attributes of exemplary school library websites . (Dissertation. University of North Texas). Retrieved from http://digital. library.unt.edu/ark:/67531/metadc3911/m1/.

Watry, P. (2007). Digital preservation theory and application: Transcontinental persistent archives testbed activity. *International Journal of Digital Curation, 2*(2), 41–68.

Chapter Nine

Dealing with Legal and Ethical Issues

School library reference and information services (RIS) surprisingly reveal a raft of legal and ethical issues. School librarians are often considered the copyright police in their role of information providers and facilitators. They probably know more about intellectual property and freedom issues than anyone else within the school community, besides lawyers, and are more likely to interact with the school community than lawyers. School librarians not only have to help their community, but they are also responsible for the library collection in terms of security and confidentiality. School librarians also strive for equitable access and treatment, modeling it and teaching it to the school community. With the advent of the Internet, ethical questions have exploded. Furthermore, because school libraries have in loco parentis status, they are more apt than other library settings to deal with ethical dilemmas. This chapter discusses these issues and suggests ways that school librarians can model and teach ethical information behavior.

LEGAL ISSUES

Several legislative acts directly impact school library RIS. School librarians should become acquainted with these laws, not only because they are responsible for complying with them—and seeing that library users also obey them—but also because some of these laws run counter to library values.

- Library Services and Technology Act (LSTA) funds all types of libraries. Its priorities include technology, underserved populations, and rural services.
- No Child Left Behind Act of 2001, which was a reauthorization of the Elementary and Secondary Education Act (ESEA), expands the federal

role in public education, particularly in the area of assessment. One of its provisions, Title I, helps fund schools with a high percentage of low-income families with students. Title I sometimes underwrites supplemental library resources and services.

- Individuals with Disabilities Education Act, Americans with Disabilities Act, and Assistive Technology Act require appropriate resources and services for these populations. For example, public documents, such as library portals, need to be accessible to the largest population possible.
- Telecommunications Act requires schools and libraries to receive low-cost telecommunications service. It also requires service providers to address accessibility issues. However, the Children's Internet Protection Act puts restrictions on the Telecommunications Act, ESEA, and LSTA in the form of requirements for Internet safety policies and techology through filtering and other blocking programs. Unfortunately, no perfect Internet filter exists, so some curricular resources may be blocked. The Brenner Center for Justice developed a valuable public policy report in information filters that can guide discussion (http://www.fepproject.org/policyreports/filters2intro.html). Required acceptable use policies are another way that school districts can show due diligence in complying with these technology legalities.
- The Family Educational Rights and Privacy Act (FERPA) protects the privacy of student education records, which includes circulation records, though there are a number of exceptions such as sharing information with school officials for legitimate educational purposes or under a subpoena or judicial order.
- The USA PATRIOT Act (Uniting and Strengthening America by Providing Appropriate Tools Required to Intercept and Obstruct Terrorism) expands law enforcement surveillance and investigative powers, including telecommunications. To a degree, this act countermands FERPA and can jeopardize intelletual freedom and privacy. The American Library Association maintains a clearinghouse of useful resources to help deal with this act: http://www.ala.org/Template.cfm?Section=ifissues&Template=/ContentManagement/ContentDisplay.cfm&ContentID=32307.

Intellectual property encompasses a variety of laws. Copyright law is the most well-known legislation in the library world because it protects intellectual property in terms of the rights and compensation of intellectual creators balanced with the needs for access to information. The Copyright Act of 1976 is the driving statute; it codifies fair use as well as describes copyright rights and limitations. The Digital Millennum Copyright Act, added in 1998, delas with technological issues, especially online material. It also addresses digital presentation and limits database company liability. The technology practices can be very complex and restrictive, as these examples demonstrate:

- Images should not be altered or resized without explicit permission.
- If made public, photographs of recognizable people require written permission.
- Sharing scanned or digitized work publicly requires prior permission.
- Music and video downloads can be problematic, particularly as different producers may give different permissions for different products.
- Depending on the company's licencing agreement, computer program appearance, graphics, and sound might be covered by copyright.
- Online slander and libel, such as on social networks, have legal and possibly criminal consequences, even for minors.

Social media practice poses even more questions: Who is the author? For documents that are dynamic, such as wikis and blogs, what is copyrighted when compensation is considered? How are mash-ups copyrights? How are file sharing entities handled; how does their copyright differ from traditional databases?

Fortunately, educational institutions enjoy more freedom in using copyrighted materials if the intent is teaching and personal research without market compensation. These fair use exemptions are listed in Section 107 of 17 United States Code 106:

1. the purpose and character of the use, including whether such use is of commercial nature or is for nonprofit educational purposes;
2. the nature of the copyrighted work;
3. amount and substantiality of the portion used in relation to the copyrighted work as a whole; and
4. the effect of the use upon the potential market for or value of the copyrighted work.

The TEACH Act of 2002 (Technology, Education and Copyright Harmonization) enables teachers to apply the same copyright practices to online learning environments as long as the resources are available only to the enrolled students for the period of the course. Several educational guidelines about copyright and fair use exist:

- American Library Association for Information Technology Policy: http://www.wo.ala.org/districtdispatch/?p=3207
- Copyright Advisory Office of Columbia University Libraries' Information Services: http://www.copyright.columbia.edu/fair-use-checklist#

- National Council of Teachers of English: http://www.ncte.org/positions/statements/fairusemedialiteracy
- Taking the Mystery Out of Copyright (Library of Congress site for teachers): http://www.loc.gov/teachers/copyrightmystery/#
- Copyright and Fair Use in the Classroom (University of Maryland): http://www.umuc.edu/library/copy.shtml
- Stanford University links on fair use: http://fairuse.stanford.edu
- University of Texas copyright crash course: http://www.lib.utsystem.edu/copyright/
- A Fair(y) Use Tale: a fun video using Disney movies to explain Fair Use (Media Education Foundation): http://www.youtube.com/watch?v=4bK8AZSYtPU

Increasingly, teacher librarians are developing repositories or databases of learning objects that are generated in-house or within the school district. These databases might include lesson plans, rubrics, "pools" of test question items, sample student work, and so forth. Open Education Resources (OER) are a subset of learning objects that are available for free. OERs are usually regulated by a Creative Commons agreement that stipulates how they may be used. Typically, educators can use and modify them as long as they credit the original authors. Educators are also encouraged to submit their modifications for others to use, crediting the changes. In this way, intellectual property is shared ethically and advances the profession quickly. Sample directories and repositories of OERs can be found at http://creativecommons.org.

RIS ETHICS AND SCHOOL LIBRARIANS

Legislation differs from ethics in that ethics reflect social norms but are not necessarily regulated by legal authorities. Laws generally enforce public acts, but unethical acts may be done in private. Especially with the continuing advances in technology, legislation has a hard time keeping up with these advances, and even ethical norms have to be negotiated. Netiquette, online manners, exemplifies the idea of behaving ethically.

School librarians encounter ethical issues daily: providing accurate information, observing intellectual property rights, dealing with privacy issues, maintaining confidential relationships with library users. The American Library Association (ALA) began talking about an ethical code in the early twentieth century, with the first code being adopted in 1939. Their core operational definition of ethics posits an "essential set of core values which define, inform, and guide our professional practice" (ALA, 2008). This Code of Ethics provides a framework to guide ethical decision making. It includes statements about excellence in service, intellectual property and freedom, collegiality, conflict of interest, and professional growth.

The school library program as a whole, and certainly RIS, should model ethical behavior and social responsibility. Hallahan (2006) identified eight ethical factors considered part of responsible public relations, which apply well to RIS and provide an ethical framework.

- Provide the school community with opportunities for access by offering a choice of technology tools and venues for communicating (e.g., e-mail, Twitter, Facebook, wikis).
- Provide accurate and consistent content, both textually and visually.
- Avoid deceptive practices such as misappropriation of other people's content, misrepresenting information, unethical tracking, and manipulating search engine ratings.
- Provide reliable and timely information and service.
- Take advantage of interactivity by fostering two-way communication and acting in response to input.
- Personalize and customize online experiences; social media provide several mechanisms.
- Ensure privacy and security.
- Supply relevant information in a format that is manageable for diverse users (e.g., posters, displays, bibliographies, videos, podcasts, web pages).

Hallahan also provided a list of useful websites that address ethics and telecommunications:

- Centre for Democracy and Technology: http://www.cdet.org
- Computer Ethics Institute: http://www.computerethicsinstitute.org
- Computer Scientists for Social Responsibility: http://www.cpsr.org
- Electronic Frontier Foundation: http://www.eff.org
- Ethics Resource Center: http://www.ethics.org
- Online Ethics Center for Engineering and Science: http://onlineethics.org
- Wired Safety: http://www.wiredsafety.org

LIBRARY POSITION STATEMENTS DEALING WITH ETHICS

While position statements do not have the authority of law, they do guide policies, which can be enforceable. The American Library Association and its units, including the American Association of School Librarians (AASL), have developed several position statements that deal with ethical issues impacting RIS. In addition, these organizations have created toolkits that gather resources to help librarians address these matters professionally.

Under the main ALA website, one can drill down the the Library Bill of Rights (http://www.ala.org/advocacy/intfreedom/librarybill), which affirms that "all libraries are forums for information and ideas, and that the following basic policies should guide their services" (p. 1). That web page links to associated position statements that impact school library RIS:

- Access for Children and Young Adults to Nonprint Materials
- Access to Digital Information Services and Networks
- Access to Library Resources and Services Regardless of Sex, Gender Identity, Gender Expression, or Sexual Orientation
- Access to Resources in the School Library Media Program
- Challenged Materials
- Diversity in Collection Development
- Economic Barriers to Information Access
- Evaluating Library Collections
- Exhibit Spaces and Bulletin Boards
- Expurgation of Library Materials
- Free Access to Libraries for Minors
- Importance of Education on Intellectual Freedom
- Labeling and Rating Systems
- Library-Initiated Programs as a Resource
- Meeting Rooms
- Minors and Internet Interactivity
- Privacy
- Restricted Access to Library Materials
- Services to Persons with Disabilities
- Universal Right to Free Expression

The ALA Office of Intellectual Freedom (http://www.ala.org/offices/oif) has position papers and other resources on academic freedom, censorhip in schools, challenges to library materials, control and censoring of the Internet, privacy and confidentiality, religion and intellectual freedom, the USA PA-TRIOT Act, and state privacy laws regarding library records. They have also packaged their information into an intellectual freedom manual, toolkit, and set of statements and guidelines.

The ALA Office for Library Advocacy has compiled ethics documents in their Advocacy University website (http://www.ala.org/advocacy/advocacy-university). They provide resources on Interent safety, special needs and underserved populations, and young adult advocacy.

The ALA Office for Literacy and Outreach Service (http://www.ala.org/offices/olos) focuses on ethical issues related to equitable access. They provide guidance for librarians to help provide RIS for GLBT people, people of color, people with disabilities, poor and homeless people, and rural and tribal populations.

The ALA Office for Information Technology Policy (http://www.ala.org/offices/oitp/) provides information on e-rate, e-books, and digital content issues. AASL developed a series of position statements that address RIS ethical practice (http://www.ala.org/aasl/advocacy/resources/position-statements):

- Common Core College- and Career-Readiness Standards
- Confidentiality of Library Records
- Digital Content and E-books in School Library Collections
- Diversity in the Organization
- Flexible Scheduling
- Reauthorization of the Elementary and Secondary Education Act
- Resource Based Instruction: Role of the School Librarian in Reading Development

AASL also developed a white paper that focuses on educational technology ethical practices in school libraries: filtering practices, acceptable use policies, apps, social media, and use of personal devices (http://www.ala.org/aasl/advocacy/resources/whitepapers/ed-tech).

EQUITY IN THE LIBRARY/MEDIA CENTER

The following study, conducted by Yung Tran, exemplifies the ethical need to address the RIS needs of all students.

A demographic profile of ABC Intermediate reveals a highly diverse, culturally rich image. The divisions are as follow: 351 students in grade seven and 301 students in grade eight from Orange County. Of this total, 41 percent are Limited English Proficient and 29 percent are Fluent English Proficient. The gender distribution is as follows: 349 male and 303 female. The ethnic distribution is as follows: American Indian .3 percent, Asian 61.2 percent, Pacific Islander .2 percent, Filipino 1.1 percent, Hispanic 18.5 percent, Black .9 percent, and White 17.8 percent. Students on free and reduced lunches make up 60 percent of the school. The school is high performing and is a California Distinguished school.

It is imperative that the school Library Media Center (LMC) must provide accommodations to serve different linguistic and cultural subgroups. In this study, I address the needs of the English language learner (ELL) students, particularly the Vietnamese since they make up a huge bulk of the school population. I have analyzed the barriers and offered some solutions. Many of the recommendations might not become reality, but it is always good to know what is possible.

Student and Family Barriers to Information

Language:

- Many speak Vietnamese at home and even at school.
- The directions/signs/labels in the LMC are in English.
- To navigate and search for information require English.
- Most of the books in the LMC are in English.

Cultural:

- Students and family afraid to seek help from "the unapproachable authority" and when seeking help, "the teacher is regarded as the repository of all knowledge; no independent investigation is required, and it may in fact be strongly discouraged" (Bopp and Smith, 2011, p. 282).
- These ELL students tend to move in "flocks," that is, they need each other for assurance. If the LMC is full of the "other" kids, let's say, Hispanic; these Vietnamese ELL students would not venture into the LMC.

Access:

- Not many students have computers at home. Even if they do, most of them would not have Internet services.
- Students lack computer skills.

LMC staffing:

- The LMC only has one school librarian (SL), who cannot be in several places at the same time.
- Teachers who bring their classes in are not very familiar with the services and design of the LMC to assist the SL.
- There are no library assistants who can speak the language.

Solutions

Language:

- Make Vietnamese language or bilingual materials available.
- Have LMC directions/signs/labels in Vietnamese.
- Have materials for teaching and learning English such as Vietnamese English dictionaries.

Cultural:

- Create a "Vietnamese corner" in the LMC.
- Announce the newly arrived Vietnamese materials on the PA or in the ELL classrooms.
- Book talk in ELL classes.
- Find books that relate to their experiences such as the refugee camps or books about Vietnam to help the homesick.
- Smile.
- Have book lists in Vietnamese.
- Smile again.
- Ask for volunteers who speak Vietnamese to help out at lunch and break.
- Learn to say, "Have a good day" in Vietnamese.
- Allow students to post their Vietnamese experience work (e.g., art or essays) in the LMC so that they have the opportunities to share experiences.

Access:

- Have lists of Vietnamese websites for different topics.
- Increase orientation for ELL students to teach them how to navigate the LMC and on the computers (with bilingual aide if possible).
- Offer evening class on technology for parents.
- Have the school website available in different languages.
- Ask parents to create AR/Scholastic Reading Counts tests for the books in Vietnamese.
- Purchase ELL software.

Staffing:

- Hire a library aide who can speak the language.
- Ask the counselor to assign more Vietnamese-speaking students to be in Library Practice.
- Do staff development services about access, especially the Vietnamese area.
- Contact the public libraries or community services that have Vietnamese information services.

- Partner with the ELL teachers in their classroom projects/assignments.

Relevant policies:
I am not aware of any school or district policies on access for underserved groups. I am also not aware of any school or district policies on making these areas accessible for disabled students.

Evaluation of Services

- Observation: how students behave from the first day to now, how long it takes for Vietnamese students to find some information, do students walk to the LMC door and then turn away, do students avoid you when they need help, can students perform searches independently after you show them the tools, etc.
- Statistics: how many of the patrons are Vietnamese, how many bilingual or Vietnamese books have been checked out, how often students take the AR/Reading Counts tests, etc.
- Teachers' survey, especially the ELL teachers: Questions can include: Have the students found enough information to satisfy the requirements of the assignments? What should be deleted from orientation? What should be added to help their students navigate the LMC?
- Informal student interview: Questions can include: What do you like to read? Are those bilingual books too hard?
- Form an advisory committee who looks at LMC services periodically (ideally students' and parents' involvement should be encouraged).

RESEARCH ETHICS

When school community members conduct research, they should act ethically. Besides copyright compliance and the larger issue of intellectual property, the following ethical issues need researchers' consideration (American Psychological Association, 2010). While these guidelines are directed to scholarly research and publication, the underlying principles apply to student research efforts as well, and school librarians should remind students how their work draws upon the larger world of research.

- Pose ethical research questions: questions should benefit society, not make conditions worse. For example, research should not be conducted in order to seek revenge on a colleague. Do not misrepresent the purpose of the research. Disclose any possible conflict of interest, such as personal gain. Get administrative approval for research that is done on the school community.

- Collect data ethically. Do not misrepresent the purpose of collecting data, unless concealment or disception is justified for the research's value (e.g, the stated purpose is to determine which websites a student uses when in reality the study intends to determine the degree that students share information about websites). Do not fabricate data. Do not use unethical means to arrive at an ethical result. Keep records safe and confidential.
- Make every effort to protect human and animal subjects, and minimize any risk. Normally, research subjects should be voluntary and give informed consent about their responsibilities and obligations. Parents or guardians need to give consent for their children to be active research participants. In educational settings, explicit permission is not needed if the research involves normal educational practice, standard tests, uninvasive surveys, observation of public behavior, collection of preexisting data, and protection of individual identity. Get explicit permission for recording people's distinguishable voices and images.
- Maintain an ethical relationship with people who will be impacted by the research. Be sensitive to other other people's concerns, such as student evaluations. Try to remain objective and not favor one person over another. Do not play "spy" for the administration. If a person asks for some information to be "off the record," either keep that commitment or do not have the person share the information. Keep confidentialities unless there is imminent danger, such as violence or suicide.
- Analyze data ethically. Any personal biases and gains (such as getting money from a commercial database company) that impact interpretation should be openly acknowledged. Data should not be twisted to support some preexisting agenda or assumption. Clarify values that enter into the analysis or interpretation.
- Report the data ethically and in a timely manner. Do not misconstrue the data, findings, discussion, or recommendations. Do not misrepresent data in statistical graphs. Acknowledge other sources of information.

TEACHING LEGAL AND ETHICAL INFORMATION BEHAVIOR

In their set of learning standards (2007), the American Association of School Librarians (AASL) explicitly state that "ethical behavior in the use of information must be taught" (p. 2). Dealing with minors adds another layer of legal issues and implies an additional need to model ethical behavior so children will experience and integrate such values. Each standard includes

dispositions, which address attitudes and beliefs that drive behavior and responsible actions.

• In thinking critically, students are expected to respect intellectual property.
• In applying and generating knowledge, students need to make ethical decisions.
• In sharing knowledge, students should use information to support democratic values and intellectual freedom.
• In pursuing personal growth, students should practice safe behaviors in
personal communication.

Digital citizenship constitutes a subset of these learning standard ethics. It
may be defined as the ability and habit of using technology safely, responsibly, critically, productively, and proactively to contribute to society. Digital
citizenship crosses curricular borders, just as information and technology
literacies do.

Having a schoolwide citizenship/ethics scope and sequence across curricular areas provides a venue for learning ethical behavior, including digital
citizenship, that links to the overall intellectual framework. Furthermore, the
school community needs to model ethics/citizenship in its infrastructure and
actions: providing equitable access to digital information, making provisions
to ensure that the school community is digitally safe, having a plan to secure
and protect educational data in case of crime or disaster, maintaining privacy
and confidentiality of individual records, creating and enforcing policies that
protect the digital rights of everyone, and training staff to keep them current
in digital citizenship education themselves.

The following four-step process can guide students in thinking about
ethical behaviors, especially in terms of digital citizenship, and ways to act.
In addition, several digital citizenship learning activities and informational
sources can be found at http://k12digitalcitizenship.wikispaces.com.

1. Awareness. Draw attention to students' personal digital informational
needs and behaviors. How often do they use the Internet? What information
do they search for? How do they ascertain the accuracy and value of information found? Use a survey to solicit students' experiences with social networking and consequences, such as embarrassment, loss of reputation, or cyberbullying. Ask them how they deal with their digital life in terms of privacy,
identity, and social support.

2. Engagement. At this point, students can learn about intellectual property and intellectual freedom laws as well as other legislation that impacts
information creation, dissemination, and use. Students need to know both
their rights as well as their responsibilities. Because technology keeps ex-
panding and changing continuously, laws are behind practice, and even so-

cial norms of behavior are dynamic. Students can examine hoax information such as http://www.museumofhoaxes.com/hoaxsites.html, http://www.hoaxbusters.org/, and http://www.snopes.com/; they can discuss how to evaluate information critically and posit possible consequences if someone acted on the false information. What responsibility should the hoaxer bear for real-life negative outcomes? When engaging with digital information from a legal or ethical standpoint, one of the most effective strategies is case studies: librarians can share legal cases and current news (e.g., homeland security, WikiLeaks, National Security Agency surveillance) dealing with technology issues that arise in access to confidential information, broadcasting inappropriate information, social networking, file transfer, pirating or plagiarizing information, and other intellectual property issues. What are the underlying ethical issues? What are the consequences? What are alternative actions that could have been taken?

3. Manipulating Information. Students can develop their own scenarios to research. As learners self-identify inappropriate digital behaviors and impacts, they become more aware of the problem. When they are involved in developing ways to solve the problem, they gain more ownership and control, feeling empowered to cope themselves as well as to help their peers. Students can also "produce" information by representing a given set of data: graphically, numerically, as a diagram, as a lab report. Similarly, they can manipulate images through cropping/selection and filtering techniques. In doing these physical and psychological manipulations, students learn how different representations can be used to influence opinion.

4. Application. How does one act on the information? That is often the ultimate real-life goal, particularly as an ethical citizen. Perhaps by analyzing available information, one decides how to vote in an election. Librarians can facilitate this proactive application by having students create position presentations for the local government or help a local group implement those recommendations; then that ethical learning can impact others. Other student-empowering activities that enable learners to apply digital citizenship skills include: reviewing digital sources, creating products for the community, capturing local oral and visual history, and training others in responsible technology use.

ETHICS ISN'T EASY

As the chapter opening states, ethical issues abound in school library RIS. Fortunately, school librarians can draw upon legislation, school policies, and professional resources to help address these issues. Nevertheless, controversies remain. Here are a dozen legal and ethical conundrums to mull over.

Often there is no one right answer; the solution has to be based on sometimes conflicting principles and practice, including one's own moral compass.

- You see a student posting a compromising picture of a classmate online.
- You see a parent volunteer typing on a child porn website.
- A teacher gives one of her students her log-in and password information and then complains that her network directory has been compromised.
- A student and his parent have not signed the school's acceptable use policy; they demand equal access to information required for a course.
- A student shows you his personal website, which has several Bugs Bunny figures.
- You see a teacher's school website, which also publicizes his personal tutoring service.
- Should you allow cookies on the computers? The feature is sometimes required for access to the desired resource but captures personal information in the process.
- A middle school student wants information on how to make beer.
- The principal wants you to remove a reference book on sexually transmitted diseases.
- The principal asks you to make thirty photocopies of an article for a faculty in-service.
- You find that the newly purchased science software is not ADA-compliant.
- You collaborate with a teacher to study the impact of a proscribed reading program, which you dislike—and fear will negatively impact purchases for the library collection. The study data finds that the reading program is very effective.

REFERENCES

American Association of School Librarians. (2007). *Standards for the 21st-century learner*. Chicago: American Library Association.

American Library Association. (2008). *Code of ethics of the American Library Association*. Chicago: American Library Association.

American Psychological Association. (2010). *Publication manual of the American Psychological Association* (6th ed.). Washington, DC: American Psychological Association.

Bopp, R., & Smith, L. (Eds.). (2011). *Reference and information services: An introduction* (4th ed.). Westport, CT: Libraries Unlimited.

Hallahan, K. (2006). Responsible online communication. In K. Fitzpatrick & C. Bronstein (Eds.), *Ethics in public relations: Responsible advocacy* (pp. 107–131). Thousand Oaks, CA: Sage.

Chapter Ten

Managing Reference and Information Services

Reference and information services (RIS) are only as effective as their management: providing the conditions for optimum programs. Resource management has already been addressed. The facility as a whole should support and encourage interaction with research information. The facility may also consist of the virtual space, which needs to be maintained as well: in terms of infrastructure, digital resources and software, cataloging, and other access to information such as web portals. School librarians also need to budget resources and optimize resource sharing. They also need to train library staff and volunteers to support reference and information services. Effective policies and procedures need to support reference and information services, which should tie back to strategic planning and assessment.

FACILITIES FOR RIS

A vibrant and inviting learning environment sets the tone for school library RIS and engaging information experiences. The library as learning commons acknowledges the importance of physical space where the school community can gain information, exchange ideas, and generate knowledge together. To that end, the school library needs to be open as much as possible, before the first class of the day through to time after the school day. In a few cases, schools may have closed campuses outside the class times or transportation might limit on-campus access, so the library might need to make arrangements with other public libraries. In any case, the school library needs to make sure that the school community can access library resources and services virtually as well as physically.

Opening the doors is just the first step. Furniture should enable users to study individually and in groups. Study carrels and table-top barriers cut down on visual distractions. Even setting individual desks next to each other in zigzag order can cut down on interaction. A desk might be set at the far end of a shelving range or in a corner "nook" to provide privacy. A table "bar" with power strip can be set against a long window so students can bring devices and study alongside each other in relative peace. Chairs can be moved to face a window rather than the center of the room to set a tone of privacy. Some libraries provide a quiet study section isolated from the rest of the library. These corners may be a challenge in terms of supervision, but if the library staff can establish a culture of differentiated space and respect for different learning needs, students will respect those spaces and monitor each others' use.

On the other hand, the library also needs to provide areas for group work, such as tables and study corners or rooms. Ideally, the library could have glassed-off study rooms. Another solution is to provide a reference area where 42" high reference shelves surround a few study group tables, separate from the rest of the collection and furniture. "Genius bars" are gaining popularity in libraries; a shared computer monitor is set at the end of a rectangular or semicircle table set with three or four chairs and a central power strip with a switcher enables students to work with their own devices and share the screen as needed. Movable whiteboards and markable areas on the wall enable students to write their ideas collaboratively.

Of course, the reference collection needs to be placed for maximum use. As noted in the resource chapter, many school librarians are integrating most of the reference resources into the general collection and maintaining a ready-reference collection in the information service area. The librarian's desk or office should be located near this area to provide quick assistance, complete with a computer that has a joint-viewing monitor screen to facilitate reference interaction. In addition, a reference-only set of computer stations or genius bar can facilitate quick consultation for individuals and small groups. If reference programs are resident in single computers and not networkable, those stations should be located in the reference area. High-profile signage alerts students to these valuable resources and services, and students might brainstorm more user-friendly terms for this area, such as "info central" or "help center." Library guides such as pathfinders, reference sheets, and research handbooks can be stocked here for quick use and as giveaways. In any case, the RIS should be easy to find and quick to access. RIS areas are usually located in the front corner across from the entrance beyond the circulation desk: easy to see yet away from the main traffic flow.

It should be noted that the reference area needs to be ADA-friendly. At least one computer station and desk needs to accommodate wheelchair access, and aisles need to be wide enough (at least a yard wide) to enable students in wheelchairs or using crutches to move through the area. At least one computer station should be set up with a trackball mouse, adjustable keyboard, scanner, larger monitor with built-in magnifer functionality, text-to-speech functionality, and headphones.

RIS TECHNOLOGY ISSUES

A robust technology infrastructure is vital for today's RIS. Digital reference resources are only as useful as the equipment needed to access them. Here is a beginning checklist of elements that need to be in place and operating dependably.

- adequate and stable power source: increasingly, schools need to ramp up their power services to handle increased electricity demands;
- adequate electrical wiring and number of electrical outlets: overdependence on power strips is not a good practice;
- means to keep cables and cords tidy and safe from being pulled out or tripped over;
- air conditioning;
- ability to support user devices brought into the library;
- emergency power supply backup;
- backup system for the library's integrated management system;
- broadband Internet connectivity and adequate network wiring for most (if not all) computer stations;
- e-rate agreement;
- if using wifi as the Internet connectivity method, having wifi repeaters and boosters to avoid signal blind spots;
- cable download site: all local cable stations are required to provide every school with at least one cable download spot;
- security systems: for the room, for each computer stations, and for each computer operating system;
- secure hardware storage area;
- backup or spare computer, monitor, external drives;
- adequate supply of labeled cables and cords;
- backup or spare technical supplies: batteries, bulbs, etc.;
- tool kit;
- emergency kit (food, water, flashlight, first aid supplies, radio, plastic sheeting, protective covering, office supplies, copies of critical files);
- disaster and data recovery system plan: see http://calpreservation.org/ for detailed resources;
- inventory and maintenance record of all equipment;

- contact information for technical assistance of equipment, software, and Internet services.

Several sources of information detail how to address these factors:

- ALA maintains a bibliography on building libraries and library additions: http://www.ala.org/tools/libfactsheets/alalibraryfactsheet11.
- ALA's Association of College and Research Libraries (ACRL) division has a wiki about planning library buildings: http://wikis.ala.org/acrl/index. php/ACRL/LLAMA_Guide_for_Architects_and_Librarians.
- The Library Design Project (http://www.librisdesign.org) developed a valuable series of library design planning documentation, including technology infrastructure design, which can be downloaded.
- ALA's Library Leadership and Management Association (LLAMA) division developed useful library security guidelines (2010) (http://www.ala. org/llama/sites/ala.org.llama/files/content/publications/ LibrarySecurityGuide.pdf).

Equipment to support RIS requires careful attention. Not only computers but other items such as camcorders, digital cameras, and televisions should be provided for in-library use and for checkout, usually to teachers. Throughout the equipment's lifetime, steps for their management should be followed (Farmer & McPhee, 2010).

Selection. Librarians should read reviews of products and identify those specifications needed to support the relevant resources. Overall, equipment should have a good maintenance record and be physically sturdy enough to withstand weather and repeated and jostled handling. Librarians should also check to see what additional items are needed; for instance, a printer might be inexpensive, but the printer's ink cartridges might be expensive—and not last long. School districts usually have a selection policy and keep a list of approved vendors. Librarians should also consult their peers and school community expert for selection advice. Whenever possible, librarians should select equipment that exists or is compatible with other in-house equipment, such as peripherals, to facilitate its use and maintenance.

Acquisitions. Sometimes librarians can purchase equipment with other librarians or school site members in order to get discount rates. Librarians should check for possible installation service and fees and accompanying warranties and service contracts. Equipment should be checked upon receipt to make sure all the parts are included and that the equipment operates correctly. For safekeeping and dirt-free maintenance, equipment should be covered and encased securely; fragile items such as camcorders should have protective padding. Items should be labeled; a chart of the equipment pieces and how to connect them can accompany the equipment and its case to help the user keep track of them and put them together properly. Each piece of equipment should be registered with the company and inventoried in terms of name, model, serial number, company, vendor, acquisition date, invoice information, warranty information, and service contact information.

Maintenance. Several precautions help keep equipment in good working order: examination of equipment upon each check-in, temperature-controlled storage (or at least free air circulation), and scheduled cleaning. Computers need extra security measures: access authentication and authorization software (usually supplied by the school), computer security software to handle attempts of changing settings, physical deterrents to theft such as locked, connected cables. Any repairs should be noted on the inventory list.

Databases pose additional management issues because of access and licensing agreements. As librarians select possible databases, they need to find out what technical specifications are required for the database to be accessible and operational, such as operating systems, interoperability, additional software, plug-ins, graphics requirements, computer speed, bandwidth demands, network requirements, authentication protocols. Databases should be ADA-compliant, and nowadays, many librarians want to make sure that the database is accessible and readable on mobile devices. In addition, each vendor—and sometimes each product—has a unique licensing agreement and options, and these agreements may vary between libraries. These contracts stipulate the number of simultaneous users, extent of access options (i.e., in-library use only on static IP addresses, on-site access, or remote access with dynamic IP addresses), fees and payment options, file transfer options, administrative options, service options, and indemnity agreements. Librarians need to read these agreements carefully and not be afraid to negotiate terms. Ringgold provides a collection of standard licenses to help library e-resource acquisitions: http://www.licensingmodels.org/.

Most school libraries have their own portals, which serve as gateways to the library's resources and services. The typical portal includes access to the library catalog (OPAC), the library's subscription databases, library-produced guides, links to digital RIS, and library information. Current practice encourages the use of blogs, widgets, interactive polls, and monitored comments. In most cases, the portal is part of the school's own portal and under the supervision of the technology specialist (who could be the librarian). In such cases, the school's network program manages installation, authentication and authorization, filtering, and other access issues. Occasionally, school websites are tightly controlled such that all changes need to be done by the technology team; however, netware and web products usually provide a means for librarians to control the library's content independently without compromising the entire network. In terms of management, these portals should be reviewed and updated frequently to ensure that links work and to attract repeat customers. For that reason, providing a few key links is usually preferable to maintaining a long list of individual resources and URLs. While it may be tempting to have student aides manage the library portal, it is better to have them check URLs and create possible content, leaving the web modification to adult library staff; even the most dependable student can be compromised by a peer, which can then jeopardize the library's online presence.

RIS STAFFING ISSUES

RIS touches every library worker; staff and volunteers must maintain the reference collection in good order, monitor its use and circulation, and help users access resources. Usually the professional school librarian provides the instruction, though other workers might help on an individual basis. The professional school librarian also develops supporting materials such as bibliographies and tutorials, though other library workers might publish and disseminate the information. Therefore, the library program director needs to work with the rest of the library worker team to identify appropriate RIS responsibilities for each position. In general, paraprofessionals can handle daily operations such as collection maintenance, freeing the professional librarian to instruct and conduct higher-level reference interaction. RIS should be considered as a team function, with each person contributing to its overall success.

Whoever does RIS-related work needs to be trained. The professional school librarian is ultimately responsible for training and performance. If one paraprofessional works in the library, the school librarian trains that person. In some cases, the top paraprofessional library staff person trains and supervises all other paraprofessional and volunteer library workers. Since the library user tends to think that everyone who works in the the library knows "everything," all library workers should have basic knowledge about RIS procedure and resources. They should get to know and use the reference collection, access online reference sources, use reference guides, use basic productivity applications, and follow usage procedures such as reserve shelves and circulation practices. Most training follows these steps:

1. The trainer demonstrates the basic skill or procedure, talking through each action.
2. The trainer breaks down the process into understandable steps. A procedures guide with step-by-step instructions and diagrams, one step per page, clarifies the process and serves as a handy check. Some trainees prefer reading a procedures guide first, while others prefer to learn by doing.

3. The trainee does each step, coached by the trainer. The trainee should be encouraged to ask questions, and the trainer should check for understanding at each step. Some trainees like to take notes or use some other mechanism to retain the new information.

4. The trainee does the complete process, preferably verbally stating each action, with the trainer observing and confirming the action or correcting it.

5. The trainer introduces variations of the procedure once the basics are performed efficiently and consistently. Issues may arise as the trainee performs the process independently; the trainee should be encouraged to ask for guidance, and the trainer should be available for just-in-time targeted training.

6. The trainer should spot-check the trainee's independent performance to make sure that it is done efficiently and effectively. The trainer should provide timely interventions to avoid the trainee learning bad habits. Occasionally, the task does not match the worker's skill set or interest. For example, a worker with severe dyslexia should not shelve. Library services are numerous enough to find a task that better fits the worker.

7. The competent trainee, who can perform the task independently, may be able to train peers or subordinates, or at least give suggestions on ways to improve the training or procedures guide. Extended aspects of the procedure, and greater autonomy or responsibility, may be added to the trainee's skill set.

Library staffing may be shared or outsourced. For instance, a textbook clerk might work in the library in the middle of the semester, which could be heavy traffic time for research papers. A technology assistant might be shared between the IT department and the library. In these cases, the school librarian needs to have a good working relationship with these workers' supervisors in order to negotiate work hours and responsibilities. The school librarian and public librarian might do some joint reference collection development or training. Again, each person's roles and responsibilities need to be clarified. Alternatively, a school district might have coordinated library services, with each site librarian contributing to a central database of reference lessons or bibliographies. In each case, each person should have a distinct task and be individually accountable, as well as coordinating the work with others to provide more extensive and valuable RIS for the entire enterprise.

RIS POLICIES AND PROCEDURES

RIS policies and procedures are usually covered by existing documentation at several possible levels: library, school, district, state, and federal. As a reminder, policies tend to be general rules and guidelines (doing the right thing), and procedures state the details for implementing the policies (doing things right). School librarians should keep a database and binder of library-related policies and procedures and review them annually for currency. Sometimes specific factors need to be added to the base policies as follows.

Selection. Indexes and other search tools are especially important. Reference resources might be more expensive than items in the general collection, but their unique scope and potential use should outweigh cost concerns. Reference books get heavy usage so they need to have sturdy binding. Because reference information may need to be very current and accessible, librarians are likely to favor digital formats that can be accessed remotely rather than acquiring print copies.

De-selection. Many reference resources need to contain current information, so they might need to be replaced more quickly than other items in the collection. Irreplaceable reference materials might be rebound rather than removed due to wear.

Circulation. Most reference materials stay in the library. The policy might allow for overnight borrowing privileges or short-term in-class use under the teacher's accountability. Equipment tends to follow the same circulation policy as reference materials.

Reference information. Should some information, or access to it, be restricted, such as personal addresses or terrorist information?

Library portal. Several policies might apply to library portals: content to be included or omitted, style guide, general access basis, administrative and other restricted access, blocking and protection policy.

Services. Who are eligible users? What kinds and levels of in-person service are acceptable; do different types of users (e.g., students, teachers, administrators) have priority? Reference interactions should be private and confidential. What kinds and levels of service are acceptable by phone and electronically? What duplicating services are acceptable?

Referrals. Under what circumstances are referrals made? Should there be any restrictions on referrals? Who has responsibility for making referrals or connecting with a referral entity? What interlibrary loan services are provided?

Instruction. What instruction and orientation services does the librarian provide? Scheduling, planning, and instruction requirements, procedures, and responsibilities need to be negotiated and clarified among the librarian, classroom teachers, and administration. To what extent should library workers help students?

Staffing. RIS staffing, training, responsibilities, and accountability should be stipulated.

Facilities. If study areas or rooms are available, what policies determine their use?

As seen above, several RIS issues may arise when considering policies and procedures. For instance, many school libraries do not have selection policies that address digital resources, which constitute a growing percentage of reference resources. In such cases, librarians need to develop relevant policies, following these steps:

1. Determine the need for the policy or procedure.
2. Determine the relationship and alignment of the potential policy to the library program, school, and district.
3. State the policy's objective.
4. Give a rationale for the policy.
5. Give examples of the policy in action.
6. Stipulate the procedure to implement the policy.
7. State how the policy will be enforced and how people will be made accountable for its enforcement.

Before writing a policy from scratch, school librarians should try to locate existing policies that meet their criteria and then adapt them with permission. School librarians should also collaborate with school community stakeholders from the beginning of identifying the need to development and final approval by the school board.

RIS FINANCES

School library RIS finances normally fall under the general library budget. However, a case may be made that these services should be identified as a separate program line. It should be cautioned, though, that parsing RIS from the rest of the library program may be difficult to do because: (1) RIS is a central and integrated aspect of the library program; and (2) components of RIS cross traditional fiscal object code lines of instructional materials, supplies and consumables, capital expenditures, and staff expenses. Nevertheless, if school librarians want to focus attention on RIS and its value, they can use a program-based budget process to delineate the return on investment for RIS.

Table 10.1. Program-Based Budget Process

	Resources	Library Staff	Skills	Other Personnel	Time	Space	Cost	Total
Reference interaction	Ready ref, library collection, online resources	School librarian	Communication, searching, literacies		3–10 minutes	Library, class, online	Labor, printing (optional), overhead	
Reference collection development: Selection	Rest of collection, reviews, peers, publisher and vendor info, budget	School librarian	Reviewing, evaluating, ordering, budgeting	Clerk enters ordering data	10 minutes to several hours	Library	Labor, cost of items ordered, shipping/handling	

When budgets are tight, RIS may suffer. Database subscriptions may have to be dropped, resulting in permanent loss of access to the omitted resources. Ready-reference materials may be replaced less frequently, resulting in out-of-date information. Concise or abridged editions of reference resources may be acquired instead of full versions, resulting in less rich and nuanced information. Paperback rather than hardback editions might be purchased, resulting in quicker wear. Resources might need to be shared across sites, which lessens their timely availability. Single copies of resources might be purchased rather than multiple ones (such as almanacs), which limits the number of users that can access the information. All of these practices can help cut down on RIS expenses, but there is a subtle cost for each of these actions.

With less federal financial support, and sometimes less state and local financial support, school libraries are pursuing more "soft" money from foundations and other granting agencies. These money sources cannot be counted upon for long-term budgeting, so their money is best spent on one-time purchases such as expensive reference books and technologies. If salaries are paid from these donors, then school librarians might consider developing a topical plan, such as STEM (science, technology, engineering, mathematics) RIS. The money would be allocated to acquiring STEM reference resources, developing reference guides and learning aids on STEM research topics, and creating lessons and tutorials to support STEM instruction. RIS for students with special needs, be they English language learners or students with learning disabilities, might also be targeted to donor groups who are interested in these populations.

SCHOOL LIBRARY PUBLIC RELATIONS AND MARKETING

Maintaining effective relationships is another priority for school librarians as they seek effective collaboration and mutual interdependence. Public relations focus on long-term interaction between an organization and its publics or, in this case, between the school library and the school community (and other user populations).

Marketing is a management function that focuses on more immediate products and services that respond to consumer wants and needs; the core is value exchange. For the school library program, the value to the school community of RIS is student achievent and the fulfillment of the school's mission; the benefit for the library is optimum use and broad-based support (including allocation of funds). The American Marketing Association (2004) defines marketing as "the activity, set of institutions, and processes for creating, communicating, delivering, and exchanging offerings that have value for customers, clients, partners, and society at large." Marketing is often confused with the idea of sales or selling. Selling focuses on the needs of the seller; marketing on the needs of the stakeholder or potential user population.

Why do school libraries need marketing? The school has so many information choices that users may be unaware of potentially well-matched options. Especially as the role of the school library is sometimes unclear, school librarians need to define their value. Marketing provides a systematic process for identifying and delivering optimal products and services.

A marketing action plan incorporates a "marketing mix," which refers to the marketing tools of product, pricing, placement (channel), and promotion (some marketers add the tool of people): the four or five Ps. These tools aid in developing an effective marketing strategy.

Products are more than boxes; they can be goods, services, places, ideas, organizations, and people. Wood (2010) noted: "When planning services, marketers must focus on delivering benefits through the appropriate combination of activities, people, facilities, and information" (p. 82). In the needs chapter, the school librarian identified cyberbullying instructional design as a potential service. This "product" development goes through the following processes to ensure its success:

1. Determine the curriculum content: cyberbullying definitions, characteristics, factors contributing to cyberbullying, its prevalence and consequences, ways to deal with it. School librarians can research existing cyberbullying curriculum (see http://k12digitalcitizenship.wikispaces.com for a list).
2. Determine the context of the curriculum: health education, civics education, language arts.
3. Identify reference resources: content-specific resources such as learning objects and Internet tutorials (see http://k12digitalcitizenship.wikispaces.com for a list), production-centric resources such as wikis and podcasting tools, task-specific reference resources such as local hotlines.
4. Determine the type of reference service: preventative, intervention, direct to the student, targeted to staff or families.
5. Determine where instruction will occur: school library, classroom, computer lab, online, via web conference, at home.
6. Develop ways to differentiate and scaffold RIS: working in pairs, extension activities, choice of projects or resources.
7. Determine and implement assessment instrument: authentic performance, podcast product, quiz, school incidence of cyberbullying.

What makes a good product/service? Performance, features, reliability, durability, aesthetics, and perceived quality all need to be considered.

Pricing strategy may seem irrelevant for school libraries, but RIS does cost. Organizations need to show good ROI (return on investment) to their corporate/institutional body. Certainly, instructional design and delivery cost time and labor. Publicizing RIS, say with printed flyers and posters, can run up a bill. Library portal development and digital resource costs can be significant. Depending on the setting of the RIS, computer lab and demonstration equipment costs can be sizable. If school librarians spend considerable time designing and publicizing a cyberbullying workshop, and pay for a lab aide to help run the reference session, a low ROI will result if only a handful of families attend.

The third part of the marketing mix is "place": how, when, where to make the library's RIS available to the target market. To do that well requires knowing how that target market accesses goods/services and understanding the external environment (including competitors) as well as the product itself and its life cycle. What value accrues along the way from its inception to its delivery? What is the flow—the logistics? For example, the tendency is to deliver cyberbullying RIS in the school library, but school librarians could conduct a web conference to be shown in the classroom. Increasingly, library instruction is done in the form of self-paced online tutorials so that learners can access RIS anywhere at their convenience, which was done for the digital citizenship professional development modules (see http://ecitizenship.csla.net/). Such online methods might be particularly appropriate to engage parents.

At the tactical point, school librarians select the tactics to communicate their marketing message and implement their strategic plan. The fourth P, promotion, calls upon the advertising "front line" and public relations tools as well as other techniques. Note that communication will change over the life cycle of the marketing initiative. Using the cyberbullying RIS marketing example, the research-stage needs assessment can serve as a promotional opportunity, leveraging surveys and interviews as ways to inform user populations of potential RIS. On the other hand, at the point of delivery, other formats such as websites and flyers are more appropriate.

The communication arena has really changed lately because of social media. For instance, viral marketing, which happens as people pass along marketing messages, has become an effective approach because of interactive telecommunications channels. The trend is to co-opt/enlist the help of the target market to identify the desired product as well as to communicate about it. School librarians should be aware that they are sharing control of the message and communication channel, so they should be prepared—are they happy with what people say on Twitter about the library's RIS? Potentially, electronic word-of-mouth may be the most effective advertisement.

Another aspect of public relations is relationship marketing, which refers to establishing and maintaining long-term relationships beyond a single marketing initiative: having loyal "customers." This approach aligns well with school library programs and reinforces the concept of lifelong learning. The underlying idea is that the library staff is interested in its clientele and addresses their information needs in a timely and professional manner. Shaik (2009) stated that three levels of relational marketing exist:

- level one: price incentive (most school libraries offer free reference services)
- level two: social bonding (well evident when user populations say "*our school library*")
- level three: developing customized programs to meet user needs (effective RIS should provide this option).

The bottom-line benefit of marketing is impact, and of course, marketing is only as effective as the product or service that it is trying to sell. Library RIS planning, as noted earlier, requires high-quality decision making and implementation. Additionally, to ensure that goals are reached, support must be present: learner support and internal marketing (getting the school community on board). The learner focus and support can be confusing: think of wanting happy learners—school librarians need to provide them with good service (e.g., reader's advisory, attractive and relevant reference material in stock, personalized reference help) to attain the goal. Those conditions apply to cyberbullying RIS in that prepared librarians, accessible materials, and good technical support must be provided. Support is also needed for the marketing aspect of the effort: clearance to conduct needs assessments, available communication channels, opportunities to inform the school community and train library staff.

STRATEGIC PLANNING AND ASSESSMENT

By now, the need for strategic RIS planning and assessment is apparent and is seen as an ongoing function. School librarians need to assess how well the library RIS program meets the needs of the educational community on a daily basis and make adjustments accordingly. From conducting a needs assessment of the school community to developing the reference collection, from collaboratively designing instruction to curating information, from training staff to budgeting, every function requires similar steps:

1. Evaluate RIS resources and services regularly.
2. Look at RIS in light of the total school program.
3. Form a steering committee to provide long-term perspective.
4. Identify and prioritize needs or gaps.

5. Set goals and objectives with short-term benchmarks.
6. Identify human and material resources needed to meet goals.
7. Identify available human and material resources, and determine how to obtain additional resources.
8. Allocate resources and monitor progress. Celebrate benchmarks.
9. Stay concrete and visible.
10. Measure impact.

Fundamentally, RIS should contribute to student academic success, both directly and indirectly by contributing to the conditions for optimum achievement: relevant curriculum, high-quality resources, positive learning environment, school personnel effectiveness, and family support. How are reference resources selected and provided by librarians, and then accessed and used by the school community? How are reference interaction, instruction, and information curation provided, and then acted upon by the school community? By having a repertoire of assessment tools, and the knowledge of when each tool is appropriate to use, librarians can address issues as they arise. Assessment tools have been mentioned in prior chapters. Here is a review list.

- observation: of individual and group information behavior, teacher instruction, classroom collections;
- shelving: quantity and types of reference materials moved;
- collection mapping of integrated reference resources and ready reference;
- circulation records by topic, population;
- content analysis: of curriculum, class assignments (i.e., teacher handouts), class visit scheduling, instructional planning documentation, sample student work (especially cited works), Internet searching history, database hits, library portal usage, library guide usage;
- reference interactions: quantity and types of reference questions, reference-fill percentages, time per question, types of users, patterns by time and day of the week;
- interviews and focus groups: of teachers, library users, library nonusers, parents about information behaviors and RIS (including by school and public libraries);
- consultation documentation: of work with school personnel, by type, extent, frequency, follow-up;
- questionnaires: about information behaviors and RIS (including by school and public libraries);
- tests and quizes: reference skills;
- school data: census data, course grades, grade point average, retention and graduation rates, standard test scores.

School librarians hope to find positive, significant relationship between RIS and student performance. For instance, if not all first-year classes get a library orientation, do those classes who participate in this activity perform better academically? In courses where teachers plan learning activities with the librarian, is student work of higher quality than in courses where no such collaboration occurs? Do students who consult the librarian while doing a research project get better grades on their products? These are just a few of the RIS-related questions that can be investigated by gathering and analyzing relevant data. The findings can then lead to recommendations to key stakeholders. School librarians can work with them to priorize needs and decide a course of action to improve RIS, thereby impacting student success.

Comparative Assessment

Assessment of the school library's RIS may be measured relative to other comparable school libraries (which is a norm-based measure) or against existing standards for RIS (which is a criterion-based measure). Such comparisons link internal efforts to external best practices and can be used to justify added resources for local RIS. For instance, if another middle school library in the same school district has twice as many databases for similar populations, then the school librarian might be able to make a case to provide the same number of databases for all middle school libraries.

The principal organization guiding RIS standards is the Reference and User Services Association (RUSA) of the American Library Association (ALA). Their website (http://www.ala.org/rusa) provides many tools to support these services: guidelines, professional tools, publications and products, and professional development. Among the guidelines are measures for general and electronic information and reference services, collection development, and services to specific user populations such as teens.

The most overarching guidelines for information services were updated in 2000 by RUSA. They address these services from the following perspectives. Added school library specifics are woven into the following description.

- Services should anticipate and meet users' information needs. To this end, the school library staff should provide complete accurate answers, information aids, instruction, and school community awareness of information sources and services. The school library staff should also refer and provide access to information outside the library's scope.
- Resources, and supporting policies, should be provided that reflect the school community and support the school library's and school's mission. The school library staff should consult outside information systems and experts to access external information sources.

- Access to RIS should include a coherent arrangement of resources, work spaces, and services. Facilities should be large enough to accommodate needs and easily navigable. The school library should provide state-of-the-art communication methods for accessing information. Hours should respond to the school community's needs, taking into consideration available financial and human resources.
- Personnel to support RIS should be available and qualified. Personnel should communicate effectively with the entire school community. Personnel should seek professional development and be supported in those efforts by the school.
- Evaluation should occur regularly to ensure effective RIS that meets the needs of the school community. School library staff should gather and analyze relevant statistics that address local and national standards of RIS.
- The ALA Code of Ethics is followed by all school library staff.

RUSA (2003) also developed professional competences for reference and user services librarians, which apply to school libraries. These competencies focus on the aspects of knowledge base, access, collaboration, promotion, and evaluation.

These standard criteria offer clear dimensions by which to measure site-based RIS. The school librarian can conduct a discrepancy analysis to identify the gap between current and target actions. For instance, does the librarian refer students to outside sources as needed? If not, then the librarian needs to determine why. Perhaps the librarian lives out of the area and does not know about community information services such as public health agencies or volunteer organizations. The librarian can then find out about these local serivces, perhaps by consulting the community's public library. It could well be that the public library maintains such a list of community services, which can be accessed via their web portal or by contacting their reference desk. With this knowledge, in the future the school librarian is more likely to make appropriate referrals to users who need that information.

The planning guide rubric shown in table 10.2, based on the library program planning guides of the American Association of School Librarians (1999, 2012), helps school librarians align RIS with the school's efforts and consider the implementation details needed to ensure success.

PLANNING FOR THE FUTURE

As school librarians assess and plan strategically, not just in response to current needs, they can systemically build top-notch RIS that can weather temporary storms and provide predictable vanguard conditions for school-wide achievement. Here is a possible scenario to aim for.

Table 10.2. Planning Guide Rubric

	TARGET	ACCEPTABLE	EMERGING
Planning Process Preparation	Includes logical key persons, clear and useful criteria, appropriate resources, thorough and feasible time frame, valid and reliable assessment methods	Includes key persons, appropriate criteria, appropriate resources, feasible time frame, valid assessment method	Lists few key persons, few and unclear criteria, inadequate resource, unrealistic time frame, inadequate assessment method
RIS Mission Statement	Memorable and appropriate, involves key stakeholders, aligns with and supports school mission	Clear and appropriate, involves other people, aligns with school mission	Unclear, done without input, ignores school mission
RIS Goals and Objectives	Goals linked to assessment and *Information Power (IP)*, effective objectives and strategies, triangulated evaluation plan	Goals linked to assessment, reasonable objectives and strategies, valid evaluation plan	Goals not linked to assessment or *IP*, vague or unrealistic objectives and strategies, inadequate evaluation plan
RIS Action Plan	Specific and clear plan of action, good alignment with prior work, reflects good use of time, has good potential of impacting the library program and student success significantly	Clear plan of action, aligns with prior work, reflects good use of time, has some potential of impacting the library program and student success	Unclear or sparse plan of action, reflects ineffective use of time, has little potential of impacting the library program or student success
Supporting Evidence and Assessment	Includes strong evidence of the plan's implementation and assessment	Includes some evidence of the plan's implementation and assessment	Includes little evidence of the plan's implementation or assessment

The year is 2020. The tech-savvy credentialed school librarian manages a busy learning commons, supported by trained paraprofessional staff, adult volunteers, and student aides. The RIS collection includes vetted student and community reference documents as well as other high-quality open source and commercial reference sources in various formats. Reference resources are projected on movable small-group screens, and the library is bustling as students collectively discover and curate knowledge to be uploaded onto the online national (or international) educational RIS Creative Commons repository. The school community uses solar- and hand-powered mobile devices to access, create, and share information worldwide. For instance, students are collaborating with peers across the world on green educational technology projects. The school community also accesses school cybrarian subject specialists from around the world. School librarians form virtual learning communities with peers and classroom teachers to develop interest-based RIS expertise and produce digital reference products for their constituents. All types of libraries and their institutions collaborate to provide seamless and relevant RIS for their communities.

On the other hand, 2020 could look like the following scenario. Students access their textbooks from their computer tablets. Some students go to the media room to borrow a tablet from the clerk, which they have to return at the end of the day. The national curriculum provides the paced readings and tests, and teachers control classroom behavior while coaching students to meet the national standards. Students who want to read for leisure download titles from online vendors. The public library is the community reading and technology safety net for the poor who do not have Internet access; the library also has a small collection of old print books that date before books could be produced and downloaded on demand. While the library is primarily staffed by technicians, some librarians who used to work in schools are now employed by the public library to provide RIS as needed.

What will be the future of school library RIS? The future is up to you.

REFERENCES

American Association of School Librarians. (2012). *A 21st-century approach to school library evaluation*. Chicago: American Library Association.
———. (1999). *A planning guide to Information Power*. Chicago: American Library Association.
American Marketing Association. (2004). Definition of marketing, retrieved from http://www.marketingpower.com/AboutAMA/Pages/DefinitionofMarketing.aspx.
Farmer, L., & McPhee, M. (2010). *Technology management handbook for school library media centers*. New York: Neal-Schuman.
Reference and User Services Association. (2003). *Professional competencies for reference and user services librarians*. Chicago: American Library Association.
———. (2000). *Guidelines for information services.* Chicago: American Library Association.
Shaik, N. (2009). Marketing strategies distance learning programs: A theoretical framework. In U. Demiray and N. Sever (Eds.), *The challenges for marketing distance education in online environments* (pp. 125–171). Anadolu, Turkey: Anadolu University.
Wood, M. (2010). *The marketing plan handbook* (4th ed.). Upper Saddle River, NJ: Prentice Hall.

Bibliography

Abrahamson, J., Fisher, K., Turner, A., Durrance, J., & Turner, T. (2008). Lay information mediary behavior uncovered: Exploring how nonprofessionals seek health information for themselves and others online. *Journal of the Medical Library Association, 96*(4), 310–323.

Agosto, D. (2011). Young adults' information behavior: What we know so far and where we need to go from here. *Journal of Research on Libraries and Young Adults, 2*(1). Retrieved from http://www.yalsa.ala.org/jrlya/2011/11/young-adults%E2%80%99-information-behavior-what-we-know-so-far-and-where-we-need-to-go-from-here/.

Agosto, D., & Hughes-Hassell, S. (2006). Toward a model of the everyday life information needs of urban teenagers, part 1: Theoretical model. *Journal of the American Society for Information Science and Technology, 57*(10), 1394–1406.

American Association for the Advancement of Science. (1999). *Dialogue on early childhood science, mathematics, and technology education.* Washington, DC: American Association for the Advancement of Science.

American Association of School Librarians. (2012). *A 21st-century approach to school library evaluation.* Chicago: American Library Association.

———. (2009). *Empowering learners: Guidelines for school library programs.* Chicago: American Library Association.

———. (2007). *Standards for the 21st-century learner.* Chicago: American Library Association.

———. (1999). *A planning guide to Information Power.* Chicago: American Library Association.

American Library Association. (2008). *Code of ethics of the American Library Association.* Chicago: American Library Association.

American Psychological Association. (2010). *Publication manual of the American Psychological Association* (6th ed.). Washington, DC: American Psychological Association.

Ames, P. (2003). The role of learning style in university students' computer attitudes: Implications relative to the effectiveness of computer-focused and computer-facilitated instruction. (Doctoral dissertation, The Claremont Graduate University). ProQuest Dissertations and Theses (AAT 3093249).

Bailey, E. (2008). Constance Mellon demonstrated that college freshmen are afraid of academic libraries. *Evidence Based Library & Information Practice, 3*(3), 94–97.

Bilal, D. (2012). Ranking, relevance judgment, and precision of information retrieval on children's queries: Evaluation of Google, Yahoo!, Bing, Yahoo! Kids, and Ask Kids. *Journal of the American Society for Information Science & Technology, 63*(9), 1879–1896.

Bopp, R., & Smith, L. (Eds.). (2011). *Reference and information services: An introduction* (4th ed.). Westport, CT: Libraries Unlimited.

Borgman, C., Hirsh, S., & Walter, V. (1995). Children's searching behavior on browsing and keyword online catalogs: The Science Library Catalog Project. *Journal of the American Society for Information Science, 46*(9), 663–684.

Branch, J. (2001). Information-seeking processes of junior high school students. *School Libraries Worldwide, 7*(1), 11–27.

Buckland, A., & Dogfrey, K. (2010). Save the time of the avatar: Canadian academic libraries using chat reference in multi-user virtual environments. *The Reference Librarian, 51*, 12–30.

Bureau of Labor Statistics. (2013). *Media and information.* Washington, DC: United States Department of Labor.

Center for Media Literacy. (2002). *Literacy for the 21st century.* Malibu, CA: Center for Media Literacy.

Chapman, E. & Pendleton, V. (1995). Knowledge gap, information-seeking and the poor. *The Reference Librarian, 49/50*, 135–145.

Constantino, R. (Ed.). (1998). *Literacy, access, and libraries among the language minority population.* Lanham, MD: Scarecrow Press.

Dali, K. (2010). Readers' advisory in public libraries and translated fiction. *The Reference Librarian, 51*, 175–188.

Dobbs, D. (2011). Beautiful brains. *National Geographic, 220*(4), 37–59.

Dresang, E. (1999). *Radical change: Books for youth in a digital age.* New York: H. W. Wilson.

Dresang, E., & Koh, K. (2009). Change theory, youth information behavior, and school libraries. *Library Trends, 58*(1), 26–50.

Duggan, M., & Brenner, J. (2013). *The demographics of social media users.* Washington, DC: Pew Research Center.

Eichorn, F. (2005). *Who owns the data?* Mustang, OK: Tate.

Eisenberg, M., & Berkowitz, R. (1990). *Information program solving: The Big Six approach to library and information skills instruction.* Norwood, NJ: Ablex.

Farmer, L. (2008). Predictors for success: Experiences of beginning and expert school librarians. In V. J. McClendon (Ed.), *Educational media and technology annual* (pp. 157–184). Westport, CT: Libraries Unlimited.

———. (2003). *Student success and library media programs.* Wetsport, CT: Libraries Unlimited.

———. (2002). Building information literacy through a whole school reform approach. *Knowledge Quest, 29*(3), 20–24.

———. (1999). *Partnerships for lifelong learning* (2nd ed.). Worthington, OH: Linworth.

Farmer, L., & McPhee, M. (2010). *Technology management handbook for school library media centers.* New York: Neal-Schuman.

Ferrer-Vinent, I. (2010). For English, Press 1: International students' language preference at the reference desk. *The Reference Librarian, 51*, 189–201.

Fisher, K., Erdelez, S., & McKechnie, L. (Eds.). (2005). *Theories of information behavior.* Medford, NJ: Information Today.

Flanagan, A., & Metzger, M. (2010). *Kids and credibility: An empirical examination of youth, digital media use, and information credibility.* Cambridge, MA: MIT Press.

Foss, E., Druin, A., Brewer, R., Lo, P., Sanchez, L., Golub, E., & Hutchinson, H. (2012). Children's search roles at home: Implications for designers, researchers, educators, and parents. *Journal of the American Society for Information Science & Technology, 63*(3), 558–573.

Gasser, U., Cortesi, S., Malik, M., & Lee, A. (2012). *Youth and digital media: From credibility to information quality.* Cambridge, MA: Berkman Center for Internet & Society.

Greene, G., & Kochhar-Bryant, C. (2003). *Pathways to successful transition for youth with disabilities.* Upper Saddle River, NJ: Merrill Prentice Hall.

Gross, M. (1999). Imposed queries in the school library media center. *Library & Information Science Research, 21*(4), 501–521.

Guth, D., & Marsh, C. (2012). *Public relations: A values-driven approach* (5th ed.). Boston: Allyn & Bacon.

Hallahan, K. (2006). Responsible online communication. In K. Fitzpatrick & C. Bronstein (Eds.), *Ethics in public relations: Responsible advocacy* (pp. 107–131). Thousand Oaks, CA: Sage.

Harris, R., & Dewdney, P. (1994). *Barriers to information.* Westport, CT: Greenwood.

He, P., & Jacobson, T. (1996). What are they doing with the Internet? *Internet Reference Services Quarterly, 1*(1), 31–51.

Head, A. (2013). Project information literacy: What can be learned about the information-seeking behavior of today's college students? *Association of College and Research Libraries Proceedings.* Chicago : Association of College and Research Libraries.

Heinström, J. (2006). Fast surfing for availability or deep diving into quality—motivation and information seeking among middle and high school students. *Information Research, 11*(4), paper 265. http://InfroamtionR.net/ir/114/paper265.html.

Henry, K. (2005). *Literacy skills and strategies while searching for information on the Interent: A comprehensive review and synthesis of research.* Storrs: University of Connecticut.

IBISWorld. (2012). *Internet traffic volume.* Wilmette, IL: IBISWorld.

International Council of Museums. (2001). *Statutes of the International Council of Museums.* Paris, France: International Council of Museums.

International Federation of Library Associations and UNESCO (2002). *School library guidelines.* Hague: IFLA.

Johnson, P. (2009). *Fundamentals of collection development and management* (2nd ed.). Chicago: American Library Association.

Kuhlthau, C. (2004). *Seeking meaning: A process approach to library and information services* (2nd ed.). Westport, CT: Libraries Unlimited.

Large, A., Nesset, V., & Beheshti, J. (2008). Children as information seekers: What researchers tell us. *New Review of Children's Literature & Librarianship, 14*(2), 121–140.

Lazonder, A., & Rouet, J. (2008). Information problem solving instruction: Some cognitive and metacognitive issues. *Computers in Human Behavior, 24*, 753–765.

Lester, J., & Van Fleet, C. (2008). Use of professional competencies and standards documents for curriculum planning in schools of library and information studies education. *Journal of Education for Library and Information Science, 49*(1), 43–69.

Levine-Clark, M., & Carter, T. (Eds.). (2013). *ALA glossary of library of information science* (4th ed.). Chicago: American Library Association.

Lien, C. (2000). Approaches to Internet searching: An analysis of student in grades 2 to 12. *Journal of Instruction Delivery Systems, 14*(3), 6–13.

Loetscher, D., & Woolls, B. (2002). *Information literacy: A review of the research* (2nd ed.). San Jose, CA: Hi Willow.

Loh, C., & Williams, M. (2003). What's in a web site? Students' perceptions. *Journal of Research on Technology in Education, 34*(3), 351–363.

Lu, Y. (2010). Children's information seeking in coping with daily-life problems: An investigation of fifth- and sixth-grade students. *Library & Information Science Research, 32*, 77–88.

Lubans, J. (1999). When students hit the surf: What kids really do on the Internet. And what they want from librarians. *School Library Journal, 45*(9), 144–147.

Madden, M., Lenhart, A., Duggan, M., Cortesi, S., & Gasser, U. (2013). *Teens and technology 2013.* Washington, DC: Pew Research Center.

McLuhan, M. (1954). *Understanding media: The extensions of man.* Cambridge, MA: MIT Press.

Meyers, E., Fisher, K., & Marcoux, E. (2009). Making sense of an information world: The everyday-life information behavior of preteens. *Library Quarterly, 79*(3), 301–341.

Miniwatts Marketing Group. (2013). *Internet world stats.* Bogota, Colombia: Miniwatts Marketing Group.

Montiel-Overall, P. (2005). A theoretical understanding of TLC. *School Libraries Worldwide, 11*(2), 24–48.

Nesset, V. (2013). Two representations of the research process: The preparing, searching, and using (PSU) and the beginning, acting and telling (BAT) models. *Library & Information Science Research, 35*(2), 97–106.

Oakleaf, M., & Owen, P. (2010). Closing the 12-13 gap: School and college librarians support-
ing 21st century learners. *Teacher Librarian, 37*(4), 52–58.
Partnership for 21st Century Skills. (2013). *Framework for 21st century learning.* Washington,
DC: Partnership for 21st Century Skills. Retrieved from http://www.p21.org/overview/
skills-framework.
Purcell, K., Brenner, J., & Rainie, L. (2012). *Search engine use 2012.* Washington, DC: Pew
Research Center.
Purcell, K., Rainie, L., Heaps A., Buchanan, J., Friedrich, L., Jacklin, A., Chen, C., Zickuhr, K.
(2012). *How teens do research in the digital world.* Pew Internet & American Life Project.
Retrieved   from   http://pewinternet.org/~/media//Files/Reports/
2012PIP_TeacherSurveyReportWithMethodology110112.pdf.
Raraigh-Hopper, J. (2010). Improving library services for distance learners: A literature review. *The Reference Librarian, 51*, 69–78.
Reference and User Services Association. (2013). *Guidelines for behavioral performance of
reference and information service providers.* Chicago: American Library Association. Retrieved from http://www.ala.org/rusa/resources/guidelines/guidelinesbehavioral.
———. (2010). *Guidelines for implementing and maintaining virtual reference services.* Chicago: American Library Association. Retrieved from http://www.ala.org/rusa/sites/ala.org.
rusa/files/content/resources/guidelines/virtual-reference-se.pdf.
———. (2008). *Definitions of reference.* Chicago: American Library Association.
———. (2007). *Guidelines for library services to teens.* Chicago: American Library Association. Retrieved from http://www.ala.org/rusa/resources/guidelines/guidelinesteens.
———. (2003). *Professional competencies for reference and user services librarians.* Chicago: American Library Association. Retrieved from http://www.ala.org/rusa/resources/
guidelines/professional.
———. (2000). *Guidelines for information services.* Chicago: American Library Association.
Rice, R., McCreadie, M., & Chang, S. (2001). *Accessing and browsing: Information and
communication.* Cambridge, MA: MIT Press.
Ross, C. (1998) Negative closure. *Reference & User Services Quarterly, 38*, 151–157.
Sarkodie-Manash, K. (Ed.). (2000). *Reference services for the adult learner.* New York: Haworth Press.
Savolainen, Reijo, & Kari, Jarkko. (2004). Placing the Internet in information source horizons.
Library and Information Science Research, 26, 415–433.
Schniederjürgen, A. (Ed.). (2007). *World guide to library, archive, and information science
education* (3rd ed.). Munich: K. G. Saur.
Schroeder, R. (2009). Both sides now: Librarians looking at information literacy from high
school and college. Tips. *Educators' Spotlight Digest, 4*(1). Retrieved from http://files.eric.
ed.gov/fulltext/EJ899891.pdf.
Shaik, N. (2009). Marketing strategies distance learning programs: A theoretical framework. In
U. Demiray and N. Sever (Eds.), *The challenges for marketing distance education in online
environments* (pp. 125–171). Anadolu, Turkey: Anadolu University.
Shenton, A. (2010). Information capture: A key element in information behaviour. *Library
Review, 59*(8), 585–595.
Shenton, A., & Dixon, P. (2004). Issues arising form youngsters' information-seeking behav-
ior. *Library & Information Science Research, 26*, 177–200.
Todd, R. (2003). Adolescents of the information age: Patterns of information seeking and use,
and implications for information professionals. *School Libraries Worldwide, 9*(2), 27–46.
Top 10 Reference Sources of the Century. (1999). *Library Journal, 124*(19), 34–38.
UNESCO Institute of Statistics. (2012). Paris, France: UNESCO.
Valenza, J. K. (2007). Discovering a descriptive taxonomy of attributes of exemplary school
library websites . (Dissertation, University of North Texas). Retrieved from http://digital.
library.unt.edu/ark:/67531/metadc3911/m1/.
Vansickle, S. (2002). Tenth graders' search knowledge and use of the web. *Knowledge Quest,
30*(4), 33–37.
Watry, P. (2007). Digital preservation theory and application: Transcontinental persistent
archives testbed activity. *International Journal of Digital Curation, 2*(2), 41–68.

Wilson, T. (Ed.). (2013). *Theory in information behaviour research.* Sheffield, UK: Eiconics.

Winters, K. (2008). *Adolescent brain development and drug abuse.* Philadelphia, PA: Treatment Research Institute.

Wood, M. (2010). *The marketing plan handbook* (4th ed.). Upper Saddle River, NJ: Prentice Hall.

Zurkowski, P. (1974). *The information service environment: Environment relationships and priorities.* Washington, DC: National Commission on Libraries and Information Science.

Index

24-7, 33, 98. *See also* reference interaction

Abrahamson, J., 25
abstracts, 58
access: equity, 117, 143–146; intellectual, 8; physical access, 7, 14, 44, 65, 77–82, 117, 119. *See also* information; librarians; technology
activity theory, 34
administrators, needs, 14–15
adults: needs, 14. *See also* administrators; collaboration; families; teachers
advocacy, 142
affective domain, 35
Agosto, D., 2, 28–29, 31
almanacs, 55. *See also* yearbooks
American Association for the Advancement of Science (AAAS), 28
American Association of School Librarians (AASL), 2, 85, 111, 112, 141, 143, 147–148, 167; guidelines for school library programs, 6
American Library Association (ALA), 18, 49, 138, 140, 141–143
American Marketing Association, 161
American Psychological Association, 146–147
Americans with Disabilities Act (ADA), 138
Ames, R., 28

assessment, 104, 114, 165–167. *See also* specific kinds of assessment (e.g., environmental scan, needs assessment, SWOT analysis)
Assistive Technology Act, 138
atlases, 55–56
attribution theory, 34
aural literacy, 42

Bailey, E., 32
Bandura, A., 34
Berkowitz, R., 43
berrypicking, 35
Big 6, 43–44, 110. *See also* information literacy
bibliographies, 41, 59, 60, 131–132, 134
biographical sources, 57–58
Bilal, D., 27
blogs, 134
Bopp, R., 144
Borgman, C., 26, 27
Branch, J., 29–30
branding, 136
Brenner, J., 1, 2
Brenner Center for Justice, 138
browsing, 82–83
Buckland, A., 101
Bureau of Labor Statistics, 1

Carter, T., 49

About the Author

Lesley Farmer, professor at California State University–Long Beach, coordinates the librarianship program. She earned her MS in library science at the University of North Carolina–Chapel Hill and received her doctorate in adult education from Temple University. Dr. Farmer has worked as a teacher-librarian in K–12 school settings as well as in public, special, and academic libraries. She serves as Special Library Association Education Division chair and editor for the IFLA School Libraries Section and Literacy and Reading Section. A frequent presenter and writer for the profession, she won ALA's 2011 Phi Beta Mu Award for library education. Dr. Farmer's research interests include digital citizenship, information literacy, assessment, collaboration, and educational technology. Her most recent books are *Instructional Design for Librarians and Information Professionals* (2011) and *Library Services for Youth with Autism Spectrum Disorders* (2013).